Starting Points:
How to Set Up and Run a Writing Workshop
— and much more

Starting Points:

How to Set Up and Run a Writing Workshop
— and much more

by
Dan Rothermel

National Middle School Association
Columbus, Ohio

National Middle School Association
4151 Executive Parkway, Suite 300
Westerville, Ohio 43081
Telephone: 1-800-528-NMSA

Copyright© 1996 by National Middle School Association.
Second Printing, January 2000

Printed in the United States of America

ISBN 1-56090-109-8   NMSA Stock Number 1233

Library of Congress Cataloging in Publication Data

Rothermel, Dan
    Starting points: how to set up and run a writing workshop/ by
Dan Rothermal.
       p.   cm.
    Includes bibliographical references.
    ISBN 1-56090-109-8 (pbk.)
    1. English language--Composition and exercises--Study and teaching (Elementary)--United States.   2. Creative writing (Secondary education)--United States.   3. Middle schools--United States.
I. Title.
LB1631.R65   1996
808' .042'0712--dc20   96-20406
                                             CIP

Dedication

For Jean and Dan Rothermel, my Mom and Dad, who encouraged me all along the way.

About the Author

Dan Rothermel is an eighth grade language arts teacher at Frisbee Middle School in Kittery, Maine. In 1993-94 he was the Teacher in Residence at the University of New Hampshire and has just been admitted to the doctoral program there in reading and writing instruction. His first book, *Sweet Dreams, Robyn*, is a collection of narrative poems about his family as they deal with his daughter Robyn's leukemia.

An inveterate traveler, with his wife Hannah and children Molly, Robyn, and Will, he drove to and then on the Alaska Highway to Fairbanks and has visited 45 other states in the last four years.

Acknowledgments

Seeking skills in the teaching of writing I found my way to the University of New Hampshire Summer Writing Program. That summer I had the good fortune to have Tom Newkirk as a seminar instructor. For the first time ever in my experience, someone talked with me about my writing in a challenging and helpful way. In addition, the teacher/writers assembled there created a community for discussion unlike anything I had known before about writing and how writing might be taught. A number of years later I returned to the Summer Writing Program and was placed in Don Graves' writing seminar, which again fostered an atmosphere for me to grow as a writer. These experiences laid the foundation and gave me the confidence to write my first book, *Sweet Dreams, Robyn*, a personal story.

Many people along the way have helped me grow as a teacher and a writer:

Lynn Nelson and Bob Osterhoudt of Arizona State University, my first mentors,

Wanda Avery and Paul Roberts, my colleagues at Frisbee Middle School in Kittery, Maine, who through our teaming and conversations rekindled my desire to teach when it wavered,

Lianne Prentice, Lin Illingworth, Kim O'Connell, Brett Stewart, and Ann Baroni, interns from the University of New Hampshire, who participated in the daily dialogue of the classroom and collaborated with me on many of these ideas,

Steve Adler, who shared Wednesday morning breakfasts at Howell's Truckstop in Kittery, Maine with me for eight years and whose weekly conversations helped me rethink, fine tune, and recommit to teaching,

John Lounsbury, my editor at National Middle School Association, who gave me the opportunity for a wider audience for my teaching ideas and whose editing ensured a better product, and

My wife Hannah, and my children Molly, Robyn, and Will, who keep me balanced, loved, and healthy.

Table of Contents

Foreword

How can we promote good writing by our students? The question begs for answers, and Dan Rothermel's *Starting Points* provides many helpful ones. The author, an experienced classroom practitioner, offers ideas that provoke thought, stimulate creativity, and engender reflection. Teachers of writing who read this book will ask themselves, "Can I do this activity?" "Is what I now do as effective as this?" "Should I do this?" These are the very questions we need to engage in as we work with our students. Rothermel offers a detailed plan for organizing a successful writing classroom. For teachers daunted by Nancie Atwell's approach to writing workshops, Rothermel's refined and modified version of it will have great appeal. He shows us how to begin and what he does — the rest is up to us.

Young adolescents need to be free of harsh criticism, scorn, derision, and negative comments that can chill or kill a budding idea. Rothermel understands this. He asserts that the primary purposes of writing are to communicate, inform, entertain, and express opinions and beliefs, "not to show that one can spell correctly or punctuate a sentence without an error." He got that right!

Calling for "habits of inquiry, diligence, and seeking quality," critically important life skills for young adolescents, Rothermel includes clear directions and explanations for several activities that celebrate writing. The importance of peer response groups ("Students who learn to give feedback look more thoughtfully at their own writing.") and public speaking activities are addressed. He supports the idea that publication is a crucial element in the writing process. Students need to know that their messages will go beyond the teacher to a wider audience. Rothermel is also not unaware of the importance of time constraints. As he so aptly put it, "Goals and deadlines are the mother of productivity."

Rothermel believes that students should work and learn together in small communities where they are known and honored. He calls for teachers to demonstrate mutual respect, delineate clear outcomes, provide dependable structures, design engaging lessons, and create classrooms that connect with the students' lives. He informs his students, "We are partners in this writing workshop." His classroom activities are based on cooperation, responsibility, and trust, important values for any age. An enthusiasm for kids shines throughout the book.

"Mastery comes with practice and rehearsal." Rothermel knows that kids learn over time. He underscores the crucial need for kids to internalize routines and systems at the beginning of the year. He also shifts the direction of communication channels in the classroom from the traditional student-to-teacher route to one that has students engaging with other students: "Students need to talk to each other without always having discussions go through me." Amen!

The author's wisdom is provocative: "Giving letter grades may be required, but habits are emphasized in the classroom. As a teacher of life skills, I am not preparing them for high school, rather for life." He continues, "Middle school students must begin to take ownership and responsibility for their writing and, ultimately, their own education."

Dan Rothermel has done thoughtful educators a service by publishing his classroom practices. Whether you are a beginning teacher or an experienced hand at the writing game, you will find much here to challenge your procedures and encounter many new approaches for interacting with students and their writing.

> — **Ross Burkhardt**
> **1995-96 President**
> **National Middle School Association**

Introduction

A Monday morning at seven-fifteen, I zip along on my Schwinn five speed down Southern Avenue's four lanes of commuter traffic to Nevitt Elementary School in Phoenix, Arizona. There, I lock the bike to the fence and head for my portable classroom sitting in a playground of dry grass, which just two years before had been a field of cotton. As I opened the classroom door, the stale smell of institutional carpeting greets me. Surrounded by walls with no windows, I notice the hum of the air conditioning unit above me.

At 8:20 my sixth graders rumble in as the day begins for me, one of America's martyrs, the self-contained elementary school teacher. These thirty-two students are representative of the one thousand Chicano, Anglo, and African American students at Nevitt. After the pledge of allegiance, a tracked group of lower performing students comes to my class for reading. Taking out their brightly colored soft cover readers, they read, answer workbook questions, and do what I say for the next hour and a half. I never rest as I answer student questions, cajole the reluctant, motivate the unwilling, and lead class discussions.

After morning recess my homeroom returns for a two minute blitz quiz of fifty multiplication facts. As an introduction to a lesson on fractions, students go to the blackboard to reduce fractions to their lowest terms. Then they begin working on fifty such fractions with their heads down, diligent as usual, as I flow from desk to desk meeting their individual needs. I conclude math time with, "Whatever you don't finish is homework," as they head out the door.

With lunch but thirty minutes away, students take out their spelling books. Ah, sweet spelling. Spelling, the morning reprieve for elementary school teachers from coast to coast. Needing a minimum of instruction and without a word of dissent, students begin writing their words five times each and putting each word in a sentence. Sometimes I wonder why they comply so willingly. Is it that the assignment is so simple that it requires the bare minimum of thinking? Or is it that my students are so conditioned by years of such spelling instruction that they believe writing their spelling words five times each is a sacred ritual, one of the keys to being a successful adult? I certainly haven't given them any reason to justify why copying these words out of context is worthwhile. Sadly, they never question me. At least when the students are working on their spelling, I can sit at my desk without interruption for almost ten minutes.

And then after lunch, it's writing time. Though I have the refuge of textbooks for all the other teaching subjects, there is no such safety net for the teaching of writing. Lacking knowledge, I rely on my ace in the hole, my deep well of enthusiasm that I will need to sell the writing assignment. "Today, I want you to write a story about being on an island with three things that are important to you. What would those three things be?"

Obediently the students take out a piece of paper, and most begin writing on demand. Standing at my desk, maintaining discipline, and catching my breath, I soon hear, "I don't know what to write." At this point I don my tight red shirt and gold cape, and bound over to help.

"Tell me what's important to you."

"Your television? Anything else?"

"Your BMX bicycle? Well that's interesting. What would you do with them on an island?" After a minute the kid says, "I see." I move on to other students who are desperately waving their hands. After five or six such rescues, the undertow of needy students sweeps me out to sea. Soon the class begins talking to each other, effectively scuttling this most dreary of disconnected writing assignments. But the worst is yet to come.

That afternoon after school the students' papers are neatly piled on the bookshelf behind my desk. For a week the papers sit there undisturbed; I find it easy to ignore them. My hesitation is born of the reality that I do not know what to do with the papers anyway. My memory of teachers' responses to my writing, which is all I have to go on, is the red ink attack. Without mercy they "awk"-ed and "frag"-ed me again and again. At first I was embarrassed at their onslaught, but in time I grew numb and did not care. All that mattered to me was that the grade at the bottom of the paper was no lower than a *C*.

Finally, I succumb to the pressure and take the stack of papers to my desk and dutifully begin reading. After two papers, I cry "Uncle," and say to myself, "These are dreadful. The stories are stupid. What a waste of time for me to read this garbage. I can't go on." Momentarily, I consider the refuge of the incompetent teacher, blame the students. But in good conscience, there is no way I could justify that tactic. A mirror shows who is responsible for this mess. Though shaking my head in defeat, I don't dwell on it much at all. As an elementary school teacher, I feel drained by the hour after hour, day after day demands of motivating and entertaining students. The stack of papers returns to the shelf, never to be seen again. Kids seldom ask for their papers; they forgot about the assignment the very next day, as well they should. I hide away in the portable classroom uncertain about myself as a teacher hoping no one notices. Unfortunately, no one does.

Not until years later in New Hampshire do I begin to have the first clue. The Summer Writing Program at the University of New Hampshire gives me my initial lessons in the teaching of writing. The following fall I introduce conferencing with students one to one. They begin to write with focus and details and develop a sense of audience and confidence.

Yet, one thing stands out from that time, how weary I became running writing workshops three times a week. I felt that teaching writing through writing workshops was solid, but I found myself looking forward to the days with no writing workshops. I needed a break from the demands of all my student writers. My fatigue made me reexamine the weekly writing workshop model. To maintain some balance in my classroom and in my life, I developed "The Ten Day Writing Workshop."

As a full-time middle school teacher myself, *Starting Points* is written for practicing teachers who find it difficult to set up and run writing workshops in their classrooms. I offer possibilities and suggestions to teachers who believe in the philosophy of the writing workshop, but can't seem to get the darn thing off the ground. I use the first person throughout the text to bring readers into my classroom to spend time with my students and me.

The Ten Day Writing Workshop has the flexibility to permit language arts teachers to teach to their passions as well as to integrate the curriculum with teammates. Subjects for writing workshops come from the curriculum of the social studies, science, and math classes. For no matter one's subject passion or the interdisciplinary connections one makes with teammates, the writing workshop teaches students to write with focus, to develop ideas and descriptions, to promote the development of the writer's emerging voice, and to apply grammar conventions. In writing workshops, students learn how to improve their writing as a result of peer response groups and teacher conferences.

The teaching of writing becomes easily manageable with The Ten Day Writing Workshop. It allows teachers to meet the writing needs of one hundred plus students while it provides time for other communication workshops. Public speaking workshops as well as small and large group work balance the sometimes overwhelming demands of week after week of writing workshops. Teachers do not have to work sixty to seventy hours per week to make the writing workshop succeed. The Ten Day Writing Workshop gives teachers of writing the opportunity to lead a balanced life within and beyond the classroom.

In the chapters following the detailed presentation of The Ten Day Writing Workshop, the reader will find the larger classroom context portrayed. Other types of workshops and related team activities are described. The seemingly tightly structured writing workshop used as an illustration will then be seen as a part of a balanced language arts program directed by one of the teachers on a team.

The last chapter is devoted to a philosophy of grading and how it is implemented together with a summary delineating characteristics of successful learning communities.

Readers will, of course, adapt and revise the procedures and rubrics presented here, but it is hoped that the specificity of the descriptions and examples will encourage teachers to institute their versions of a Ten Day Writing Workshop and related activities. ✎

—1—
The Ten Day Writing Workshop

OVERVIEW

Writing in each of my five middle school language arts classes is based on the Ten Day Writing Workshop, give or take a day or two – sometimes three. The theme or focus of the writing workshop described in detail in this chapter is persuasive writing and is an example of the writing workshop plan. The schedule for the Ten Day Writing Workshop might look like this.

Days 1-3	Writing experiments
Day 4	First draft writing
Day 5	Peer response groups
Day 6	Peer response groups and teacher conferences
Day 7	Teacher conferences
Day 7	After school "catch-up" writing session
Day 8	Teacher conferences and writing is due
Day 8	After school scoring of writing folders
Day 9	Conferencing with students on their scoring rubric
Day 10	Publishing

On Days 1, 2, and 3 exploratory and experimental writing exercises are introduced with a reading to spark writing or a class discussion followed by writing. Sometimes students write on a prompt of mine and see if it yields a writing subject. On Day 4 students pick writing goals, review the scoring rubric, and select one experiment to take through the drafting process. Days 5 and 6 are set aside for finishing first drafts, holding peer response groups, and writing second drafts. On Days 7 and 8 students have teacher conferences and write third drafts, knowing that writing is due at the end of Day 8. After school on Day 7, an "After School Catch-up Session" allows students to have extra time to meet the writing workshop deadline. After school on Day 8, writing folders are scored using a rubric. On Day 9, or as soon as I have finished scoring the rubrics, conferences on writing folders are held. Day 10 is reserved for celebrating writing as students

1

read their pieces to classmates or publish them for a wider audience.

All students do not follow this schedule neatly or cleanly. The routine of the Ten Day Writing Workshop (TDWW) works for most students and allows teachers to concentrate their energies on meeting the writing needs of students over a short period of time. When workshops last six weeks or so, students write for three days, read on other days, have discussions, or give speeches. My experience is that students can sustain the emotional and academic commitment to writing for two or three weeks, but after that, they grow tired and need a change. In contrast, during the TDWW students can sustain their excitement and enthusiasm for writing. Once the writing workshop is completed, students practice and demonstrate other communication skills, present speeches, memorize and recite selections from literature or poems, have class meetings, and engage in small group work. After a week or two of other communication activities, we launch into another writing workshop. The TDWW helps students plan and budget time. A deadline that is a few days away, not weeks away, keeps students focused, engaged, and productive.

Themes of the writing workshops are often ones I select. Unless guided thoughtfully, students are likely to choose topics and styles of writing that are safe, have little intellectual risk involved, or have amused classmates in the past. When workshop themes are chosen by the teacher, students experiment with a variety of genres and expand their writing repertoire. Within the themes there are many writing choices for students. Some writing workshops that I plan are:

a.	advice giving	g.	observation
b.	biography	h.	persuasive
c.	fiction	i.	playwriting
d.	freedom, rules, and ethics	j.	poetry
e.	historical fiction from research	k.	relationships
f.	hometown heroes	l.	student choice

The writing workshop becomes a journey of self-discovery for students and teachers. Still, unexamined assumptions about the teaching of writing can sabotage and discourage teachers new to the writing workshop. The accompanying quiz is designed to provide readers an opportunity to examine their beliefs about the teaching of writing to young adolescents and rethink their classroom practice.

THE TEN DAY WRITING WORKSHOP TRUE/FALSE QUIZ

T F 1. A good critique of student writing is worth a thousand words of encouragement.

T F 2. Most students have the ability to organize their time in the writing workshop and meet all deadlines.

T F 3. Allowing students the opportunity to experiment with writing, before they must select a subject to carry forward to a final draft, is absolutely essential.

T F 4. Teachers do not have time to write with their students, and teachers who read their writing to students are wasting time and taking an ego trip.

T F 5. Reading aloud is of marginal use to middle schoolers.

T F 6. Publishing students' writing is fine in theory, but is rarely worth the trouble.

T F 7. Peer feedback is time-consuming and usually a waste of time.

T F 8. It is the teacher's responsibility to correct every mistake on every student's piece.

T F 9. Final drafts must be in pen, period.

T F 10. To conduct a writing workshop you have to be a "super teacher."

ANSWERS TO THE TEN DAY WRITING WORKSHOP TRUE/FALSE QUIZ

1. **A good critique of student writing is worth a thousand words of encouragement.** *False.*

   Student writers are vulnerable and uncertain. A "safe" classroom atmosphere must exist for writers to grow and develop. Good writing comes with experimenting and taking risks. Even well-intended critiques can extinguish the flame of young writers.

2. **Most students have the ability to organize their time in the writing workshop and meet all deadlines.** *False.*

   Such students exist in fiction or in some other school. Adults as well as middle school students can become proficient at avoidance. Structure helps students produce.

3. **Allowing students the opportunity to experiment with writing, before they must select a subject to carry forward to a final draft, is absolutely essential.** *True.*

   Warm-up writing is essential to the success of any writing workshop. Students need to see that they do not have to take every piece of writing they begin to a final draft. Some experiments in writing are not meant to see the light of day.

4. **Teachers do not have time to write with their students, and teachers who read their writing to students are wasting time and taking an ego trip.** *False.*

   All teachers who run writing workshops should write and read their writing to students regularly. Such risk-taking by teachers opens up students to a range of possibilities in writing that they might never have recognized before. When teachers write with and for the students they send the strongest message possible that writing is important.

5. **Reading aloud is for little kids, but of marginal use to middle schoolers.** *False.*

Reading aloud quietly permits writers to hear if their writing sounds right and whether words have been left out. It is the number one way to improve the skills of self-editing.

6. **Publishing students' writing is fine in theory, but is rarely worth the trouble.** *False.*

Publishing ties the ribbon on the writing package. A sense of audience is important in improving writing skills. Writing a piece solely for the teacher's examination rarely results in quality.

7. **Peer feedback is time consuming and usually a waste of time.** *False.*

In fact, teachers need peer feedback more than they can imagine. Without it, teachers will die on the vine trying to meet all the conferencing needs of their students. If teachers train students well in the art of response, they will be able to lead a balanced life in and out of the classroom.

8. **It is the teacher's responsibility to correct every mistake on every student's piece.** *False.*

To what end? Such autopsies on writing are largely ignored by students. On a marked up final draft all most students look at is the grade. And where does the teacher find the time required to scrutinize every bit of student writing?

9. **Final drafts must be in pen, period.** *False.*

If you travel this road, you are on the main line for trouble. When students must rewrite a piece because of a handwriting error or two, they will learn to hate writing. Number 2 pencils with erasers are essential tools. Word processors are also helpful.

10. **To conduct a writing workshop you have to be a "super teacher."** *False.*

Teachers just need to learn the skills of managing a writing workshop. A successful workshop is not the entire responsibility of the teacher. Students must pull their weight, too. The Ten Day Writing Workshop provides a framework in which students learn the self-discipline, the commitment, and the engagement that all writers need.

Day 1

Writing Experiments

W hen creating a writing workshop, outcomes that students should be able to demonstrate must be clearly identified. For the persuasive writing workshop, they are: (1) to develop a sense of ownership in writing, (2) to create an atmosphere of trust within the classroom, (3) to collaborate and cooperate, and (4) to learn the routines of the writing workshop.

In addition to the long-term workshop outcomes, daily outcomes are written on the blackboard each morning. These objectives give students a clear idea what they must accomplish during the class period ahead. These outcomes encourage good behavior and create an atmosphere wherein students learn the new routines of the writing workshop. On Day 1 the daily outcomes are: (1) to participate in the class meeting, (2) to listen without distraction to the story, (3) to write for ten minutes, and (4) to point after the ten minute writing experiment (pointing is telling the writer something the listener likes about the piece). Finally, an essential question is written on the blackboard to focus the lesson. *How do I interest an audience in my writing?* Students are expected to earn an *A* or *B* for the daily outcomes. If students do not, they receive an *incomplete*, rather than a low or failing grade. This incomplete is then made up some other time or after school. (See Chapter 3, Success-Oriented Grading, for details)

At the start of the period I take a set of index cards, each with a student's name, and shuffle them in front of the class. This convinces students of the randomness of the grouping. The first three cards off the top of the deck comprise one group. This group sits together in a cluster. The next three form another cluster, and so on. These clusters of desks are positioned on the edges of the classroom, leaving a center space for class meetings. Though, initially, there is some groaning over the seating arrangement, the students, in time, accept the fairness of the process. When asked why groups are formed in this manner, I explain that when students pick their groups, they select from among a small group of friends and often someone is not picked at all. If that occurs the neglected student is further isolated and the sense of community in the classroom is damaged. Equally important, shuffling cards gets new students into groups and achieves the goal of knowing well and learning from everyone in the class. Once the students are seated they may shift their desks enough so that they can see the blackboard since they are not yet ready for group work.

Then a class meeting is called. Students bring their chairs and sit with me in a circle. (See Chapter 2, Class Meetings) I then provide an opportunity for students to "check in." This one to four minute time period at the start allows students to bring up any issues or questions, especially those ones unrelated to the lesson at hand (e.g., "When is the next dance?" or "Why were you out yesterday?"). If such questions are addressed at the beginning of the period, they won't be distractions later. This time is sometimes used to discuss a major current event.

After the "check in" I read Shirley Jackson's *The Lottery*. I literally gather the students as close around my feet as possible to create an atmosphere of intimacy. Sitting on a student's desk to facilitate making eye contact with all my students, I ask them to predict what the story might be about from the title. Then the show begins. Scanning the class before I read a single word draws their attention to me. Quietly, I start, looking up every few words. My energy is maintained by zeroing in on those students who return my eye contact. Pausing often to maintain the spell allows the words to linger. Changing my voice to take on the different roles of the characters builds interest.

Once the reading of *The Lottery* is completed, the guidelines for the experiment in writing are explained using a chart on the blackboard.

Writing Experiments

1. write for ten minutes
2. begin a story or an opinion that you are not expected to finish
3. write with details
4. keep the pen or pencil moving

There are two choices for today's writing experiment. One, students may write a letter to the town council of Shirley Jackson's unnamed New England town to persuade them to keep the lottery or do away with it. (Most middle schoolers are incredulous at the ending of *The Lottery* and choose the latter option.) Two, they may choose to put themselves and their family into this story as if they are members of that community. They write how the members of their family might have reacted to this tradition of an annual lottery. Either writing experiment might be the one that students eventually choose to take through the drafting process.

Students are told that when scoring the papers I will look to see if they wrote for ten minutes. Spelling and grammar conventions are not addressed at this time. I am most interested now in having students concentrate on what they think and putting those thoughts on paper. It is, however, important to "clean up" (apply the rules of grammar and spelling) a final draft. Spelling and grammar conventions have importance so that written communication is clear and understandable. In addition, the writing experiment is an opportunity for lower-performing students to see themselves as successful. If they meet the ten minute criteria, they too deserve the *A* or *B*. Motivating and encouraging student writers so they come to class each day thinking of themselves as successful is fundamental. Once they taste success, they will write again and again. It is important for teachers not to put the cart before the horse when teaching writing skills. The primary purposes of writing are to communicate, inform, entertain, and express opinions and beliefs, not to show that one can spell correctly or punctuate a sentence without error.

Students then return to their separated desks as the egg timer is set for ten minutes. I plant myself in the center of the classroom and write. As the dominant model for writing in the classroom, students, consciously or subconsciously, note what I am doing. Clearly, teachers who write with their students have a head start on other teachers of writing. When teachers write about the subject at hand, they get a feel for the writing assignment, can judge if it is well conceived or not, and are reminded of the challenges and complexities of writing well. When I write

When students write, so does the teacher.

descriptively, with humor, or with strong emotion, my writing serves as a model for my students. If I use dialogue to bring characters to life, students will become aware of the greater number of choices they have in their own writing. When writing is seen as being full of possibilities, the creative, inventive sides of students come out. Such writing allows the students' voices (their personalities) to emerge.

When the egg timer rings, a class meeting begins for the reading of the writing experiments. Before students read, there is a mini-lesson on pointing, sharing with the writer something you like about the piece. Pointing creates an atmosphere of trust and community within the classroom. Students begin their sentences with "I like..." and then say why. Some possibilities for pointing comments follw "I like...

1. the lead. It... "
2. the ending. It... "
3. the dialog. "It makes me... (e.g., ...feel like I was there.")
4. the subject. It... "
5. the humorous language or situation in the (e.g., "second paragraph")
6. the title. It... "
7. the strong emotion shown by a character. He/she was... "
8. the realistic action of... "
9. the surprise element when... "
10. the use of the word... "
11. the phrase... "
12. the detail when you described... "

When students are first introduced to the writing workshop, they need many opportunities to practice pointing, for it does not come naturally. Initially, it is beneficial to teach pointing in a large group setting. The class meeting setting allows the teacher to model appropriate pointing comments for all students to hear. Further, the class meeting allows students to try out pointing in a safe setting in which the teacher supports and builds on the students' comments. The two part structure of the pointing encourages the students to be specific when they point.

I read my writing experiment first, and have students point. Reading my writing and exposing my vulnerability is a key first step in our class becoming a community of writers. After I open up, students are more willing to risk themselves. For example, for this writing experiment I wrote,

> As I stood in the back of the crowd, I knew that I was not going to go quietly if I were selected. Rubbing my left hand in my right, I took on a whole new personality on the day of the lottery. My teeth never showed as my lips pressed together and my eyes narrowed. I didn't talk to anyone and only nodded when eye contact was made. I folded my arms across my chest. But still I was there. I had this gnawing within me for two years now that this lottery was wrong, dead wrong. And yet, I didn't say anything. I just melted into the crowd. And as long as my family or I wasn't picked, I didn't protest. It had been years since I had thrown a stone, but still I didn't protest,

except with my body language. And my body language hadn't changed a single thing in this town.

After my piece is read and students point, then students volunteer to read their writing experiments. Once a student reads, I begin the pointing and then have classmates point. Reading is always voluntary. There is writing we all do that we do not want others to see or hear for a variety of reasons (e.g., our self-doubts, our fears about its reception, or our past experience with heavy handed "constructive criticism"). Writing exposes students' beliefs and values. Some students are not ready to be so naked and vulnerable. I check on a list of those students who point and put a star next to the names of those who help me teach by reading to their classmates.

At the end of the period all the writing experiments are collected with the spiral notebooks they all write in opened to the page of the writing experiment. This speeds up the grading process. Student writing is merely skimmed, since ten minutes of writing is all that is checked. There is no reason to read these writing experiments in depth, for they may not be the pieces that students choose to take through the drafting process. All papers are checked after school so that tomorrow I can tell the students their good grades which in turn encourages more writing. If students earn incompletes, they know that they have more writing to do, and I will help them. We arrange a time together for those students to complete their writing.

Day 2

Writing Experiments

Before class begins, the following daily outcomes are on the board: (1) to participate in brainstorming, and (2) to work in small groups successfully. The essential question for the day is: *From where do ideas come?*

Students gather for the "check in." After sharing the grades from yesterday based on the daily outcomes, I note that students who wrote for ten minutes earned a *B*, and explain what it took for students to earn an *A*. (Keep in mind that the focus of this workshop is persuasive writing.) *Passion* is the first point to be written on the blackboard. Those who write with passion write with strong and emotional language. *Details* is next to emphasize that students who write in such detail write so readers feel they are right there in the scene. Third, vivid words such as *barbaric* and *senseless slaughter* are noted as they bring up descriptive pictures in the reader's mind. Next, *suggestions* is listed since students who come up with specific suggestions and solutions are thinking analytically. Finally, *creative ideas* is added to the list. Unusual and surprising ideas show me that they are thinking. With the permission of student writers, a few writing experiments from yesterday are read to emphasize particular points of writing.

Writing experiments, like all aspects of the *Starting Points* classroom, need to be repeated and practiced for students to improve as writers. A school year cannot be a series of introductions to this writing lesson or to that point of grammar. Mastery comes with practice and rehearsal. It is often assumed that most students come to middle school knowing how to write with focus and development as well as knowing how to paragraph correctly and write complete sentences. Unfortunately, many enter middle school without such basic writing skills.

Further, appropriate composition and convention writing outcomes are selected to extend their skills and effectiveness in writing. These yearly writing outcomes give focus to each writing workshop conducted. Yearly composition writing outcomes can be to write with focus, write with development, and establish a writer's voice. Yearly convention writing outcomes can include proper paragraphing, writing in complete sentences, and correct spelling. If some students have already demonstrated mastery of all these writing tasks, we confer with them to agree upon some individually appropriate ones.

At the class meeting students suggest ideas to improve life at Frisbee Middle School, across the United States, and in the world. Their ideas are written on half sheets of paper and taped to the classroom wall. Brainstorming provides as many ideas as possible without students evaluating them, be it positively or negatively. Brainstorming starts with one idea which leads to another, then to a third, etc. Students fill the blackboard with forty to sixty ideas in fifteen minutes. Some of the changes students always seem to suggest are listed on page 11.

Students go back to their clusters of three to reach consensus on five changes that their group wants for our school and five changes for the town. They select a recorder and a presenter and work for ten minutes. Small groupwork promotes the critical skills of collaboration and decision making.

Changes at school	Changes in town
1. lockers	1. more malls
2. showers after gym	2. fewer malls
3. a later time for school to start	3. a skating rink
4. foreign language classes	4. a teen hang-out center
5. better lunches	5. no taxes
6. no detentions	6. better schools
7. more time between classes	7. lower driving age (to fourteen)
8. physical education every day	8. more arcades
9. more intramurals	9. an amusement park
10. more dances	10. a larger swimming pool

During this time I observe group dynamics and individual body language in order to asses each group's efforts in meeting the daily outcome of successful work in a small group. Placing myself on the edge of the classroom I scan the classroom for blocked groups. When one is spotted, I resist the temptation to solve the problem. In due time, I go over to the blocked group to see what is up and how I might help. Often such groups just need a little personal attention.

In a non-threatening setting, the small groups make possible the first crack in many students' bubble of shyness. These groups allow kids to talk purposefully together. By establishing small groups in the beginning of the year, the message is sent that this truly will be a class where students talk and talk regularly. It is not my role to dominate or entertain all period long. I do not have the energy to do that, even if it were desirable. Students need to talk to each other without always having discussions go through me. It is also important for me to incorporate class time to reflect and to observe the classroom activity. These "less involved" times recharge me for the more active roles later in the day.

When the class meeting reconvenes, the presenters share their group's ideas. By the end of the day there are some two hundred ideas taped to the walls. Many ideas repeat, but it creates a stimulating setting for tomorrow's writing when the wall proudly displays every one of the ideas. For grading, I note the check marks made beside the names of students who offered up ideas during the brainstorming session and combine that information with their small group grade to determine a daily grade.

Day 3

Writing Experiments

Students entering the classroom for Day 3 check the blackboard to see what to bring to the class meeting. Before they bring themselves to the class meeting, they place their bookbags and backpacks in a four foot by four foot corner that is marked off with masking tape. Having such a place keeps the spaces around desks clear for student movement and teacher conferencing. Students observe that the two daily outcomes are: (1) to write for ten minutes, and (2) participate fully in the class meeting. The essential question is *What matters to me?*

As usual, the class begins with a "check in" that allows students to make the transition from the conversation and movement of the hallways to the getting-down-to-business of the classroom. Afterward, the Day 2 grades, mostly *A*'s and *B*'s, are read. Students begin today's class thinking of themselves as successful. When they feel that way, getting them to write is simple.

At this point students check the walls and select one of the ideas or select their fiction generated from the reading of *The Lottery*. Soon they are drawn back to the class meeting to state their topic which I note on the list of student names. If some students are not sure, they pass. Before they leave the class meeting they must give me one idea they will try. Indecision, avoidance, and seeking the "perfect" choice sabotage writing and leave students with an empty sheet of paper after ten minutes.

Next the concept of audience is introduced. The writing exercise is not just for the sake of writing, but to address an audience who can bring about the change they are advocating. Further, three suggestions to consider as they write are placed on the blackboard.

1. Write all the reasons you can why the change is a good idea.
2. Write how this change might be accomplished.
3. If after writing for a few minutes it turns out you are going nowhere, skip a few lines and choose another focus to write on.

Before the students return to their desks to write, they are reminded that they each need to earn an *A* or a *B* that will be determined by their writing for ten minutes. If students earn an *I* (incomplete), they conference with me to determine whether they do not understand, are resistant to writing, or can identify some other reason why they have not written. The *I*'s are excellent diagnostic tools for teachers to determine what the individual needs of the students are. Giving an *F* is a simplistic rationalization by the teacher that students just do not care.

Students return to their desks, which have been separated and are all facing the front blackboard to minimize distractions. Again, and most importantly, I take an empty desk to the center of the classroom and write myself. The egg timer is set for ten minutes, and we all write. After a few minutes I check the list of students to note the ones who received incompletes for the first writing experiments and see if these students are writing. Only after five minutes do I go to someone who is not writing. I might ask, "What's your focus?" If that leads nowhere, I might make a suggestion or ask the student questions to get the thinking started. The student knows that if the first topic proves to be a dead end, another one can be selected. And then I leave. If my suggestions fall on deaf ears, we will meet later to make up the incomplete. I come to a student to help, not to make him/her write, since I cannot really make a student write. Middle school students must begin to take ownership and responsibility for their writing and, ultimately, their own education.

Once the egg timer rings the students come to a class meeting to share some writing experiments. Again I begin with mine.

> Focus – more physical education at Frisbee Middle School. Audience – the principal. Is your memory so short that you don't remember sitting all day in class and wishing you were outside? Kids haven't changed. They look longingly out our big beautiful windows. "Why do I spend all day sitting at my desk when the fields call?" Some students in the middle school have physical education once a week. We, a nation of couch potatoes, are not teaching the students of the 21st century how to stay healthy and fit as adults. The message we have for kids is that we don't value physical fitness, a healthy life-style, or an active life. Students need physical education everyday. That's right, every day. A full-time...

Once the reading is done students point and say what they like about the writing. When that is completed, volunteers read their writing experiments. On this second day of writing experiments students volunteer readily. They are beginning to realize that it feels pretty good to have classmates pointing for them. If there are many volunteers to read and just a few minutes left in the class period, students match up with a partner and read their piece to that partner, which gets everyone involved. When one of the partners finishes reading, the other one reads. After each reading, students point for each other. Too often, there is much excitement that comes from student writing, and yet only a few students get to read before the class period ends. Often students are pleased with their writing and want to read it to someone. If a few are able to read, others dressed for the ball have no place to go. Developing student enthusiasm for writing is important, so reading between partners is valuable.

All the ten minute writing experiments are again evaluated. A review of these papers provides many mini-lesson ideas. These days of experimental writing prepare students to begin writing a first draft come Day 4. Students have been given enough time to value their writing. Sufficient preparation is a down payment on a successful writing workshop. Writing experiments give students time to develop the capacity to care about a topic, and students learn when students care.

Day 4

First Draft Writing

Before students arrive for class, the desks are separated for first draft writing. The students check the blackboard to see that they need paper, pen or pencil, and something hard to write on (needed because students bring their chairs to the class meeting circle and write on their laps). The essential question is: *What rich details bring a story to life?* They also see that the daily outcomes are to: (1) complete the goal writing, (2) ask questions about the scoring rubric, and (3) begin a first draft of a persuasive piece

In the class meeting students "check in" and comment on a current event topic. From any of their writing experiments in their folder or from an entirely new idea on the wall, they then choose a subject about which to convince or persuade an audience. They are expected to write at least three drafts during the writing workshop, since it is important to learn such habits of writers as:

1. experimenting with words and sentences,
2. reexamining and reflecting on ideas and phrasing, and
3. learning from other students as well as the teacher.

A Goal Writing Sheet (p. 16) and a list of Suggestions for Goal Writing Choices (p. 17) are then passed out.

GOAL WRITING SHEET FOR STUDENTS

Goals for _____Writing Workshop

Name_____Section_____Date_____

Write goals in sentences.

Goal #1 -

Goal #2 -

Goal #3 -

The scoring rubric (shown on p. 18) which is more descriptive than check marks or letter grades is explained next. It gives students a clearer and more specific idea of what will make them better writers. Further clarification of the rubric categories is done during individual teacher conferences.

Throughout the school year developing good habits is a matter of primary importance for students. The habits of inquiry, diligence, and seeking quality serve students well no matter their future education or life direction. Thinking, asking questions, and seeking answers all demonstrate inquiry. Dedication and perseverance describe diligence. Substance and beauty are indications of quality. Giving letter grades may be required, but habits are emphasized in the classroom. As a teacher of life skills, I am not preparing them for high school, rather for life.

Next, their attention is drawn to the chart of "Writing Workshop Rules" (shown on p. 19) adapted from Nancie Atwell (1988) to fit the needs of our students.

During the first writing workshop of the year, more time is needed to review the goal writing sheet, the scoring rubric, and the workshop rules. It may be that what is planned for Day 4 will have to be extended over two days. In subsequent workshops, these explanations will not need to be explained in such detail.

Students' attention is then drawn to the Persuasive Writing Workshop Guidelines chart (p. 20). It suggests ideas for students to consider as they write their first draft. The need for a pay phone in the school is an example that students can relate to. Raising money to fund the idea is not something that should concern them. If the School Committee or Town Council thinks it is a good idea, they will come up with the money.

SUGGESTIONS FOR GOAL WRITING CHOICES*

1. Narrow the focus of your piece. Stick to one topic.
2. Give more specific information to develop your story so readers can see, hear, and feel your stories – more conversation and description of actions, thoughts, and feelings help.
3. Make more use of direct quotes, bringing speakers to life, rather than paraphrasing their words.
4. Punctuate quotes correctly.
5. Proofread; check for missing words and confusing explanations.
6. Draft in paragraphs.
7. Watch for too many paragraphs.
8. Conference with the teacher more often.
9. Conference with a peer at least once.
10. Complete all drafts.
11. Meet all deadlines.
12. Use all conventions correctly.
13. Experiment with alternatives. Try several different leads, conclusions or titles; then choose and work with your best.
14. Confer with yourself more often, trying to be more independent in deciding what works and what needs more work.
15. Spend more time at home on your writing: at least _____ evenings per week.
16. Work at organizing yourself. Take time at the end of each class to straighten your folder and decide what homework you have.
17. Take more time and care with final copies.
18. Work on better handwriting in the final draft.
19. Watch for comma splices. Start a new sentence or, when appropriate, use a semi-colon.
20. Self-edit for spelling by circling any words that you are not sure how to spell correctly and then look up those words.
21. Show excellent work habits each day.
22. Look at the assignment from a different point of view and challenge yourself to write it.
23. Select your own personal writing goals.

*Some thoughts from Nancie Atwell's *In The Middle* with additions.

WRITING WORKSHOP RUBRIC

Name_____Section_____

Incomplete	Basic	Proficient	Distinctive

1. FOCUS AND DEVELOPMENT

Incomplete	Basic	Proficient	Distinctive
___ no focus minimal development	___clear focus sufficient details	___clear focus detailed description	___clear focus many details reflective insights

2. CONVENTIONS OF GRAMMAR

Incomplete	Basic	Proficient	Distinctive
___improper paragraphs and sentences	___correct paragraphs and sentences	___developed paragraphs, varied sentence structure	___many developed paragraphs, dialog, sophisticated sentences

3. SPELLING

Incomplete	Basic	Proficient	Distinctive
___spelling errors	___1-2 spelling errors	___no spelling errors	___challenging words spelled correctly

4. TEACHER CONFERENCES

Incomplete	Basic	Proficient	Distinctive
___poorly written questions, speaks up little, unprepared, second draft looks like first	___asks satisfactory questions, responds to questions with details, some revision	___asks focused and specific questions, conference is a conversation, much revision	___detailed questions, clear idea where writer needs help, true dialogue, extensive revision

5. PEER CONFERENCES AND/OR PEER RESPONSE GROUPS

Incomplete	Basic	Proficient	Distinctive
___poorly written questions, speaks up little, unprepared	___asks satisfactory questions, responds to peer questions with details	___asks focused and specific questions, conference is a conversation	___detailed questions, clear idea where writer needs help, true dialogue

HABITS

1. Inquiry

2. Diligence

3. Quality

_____
Reviewer

ADDITIONAL FACTORS	___met deadline	___challenged self	___student additions

WRITING WORKSHOP RULES

1. **No erasing, except on final draft.** Following this rule is a great time saver for students in the initial stages of drafting. On the other hand, erasing on the final draft saves time since it allows students to erase an errant comma or a misspelled word without having to rewrite the entire piece.

2. **Write on one side of the paper only.** During conferences with students the pages are spread out so several sheets can be seen at once.

3. **Use pencil or pen.** Until there are computers for all students and they have satisfactory keyboarding skills, writing in pencil is acceptable for all drafts. Drafts must be legible and neat. When students can erase on a final draft, they see that the TDWW emphasizes writing instead of copying.

4. **Print or write in cursive.** Writing in cursive is a tradition that needs reexamination. Student textbooks, reading books, and words on the computer screen are all printed. Once students are in middle school they have had enough handwriting practice to last a lifetime. Students learn that the TDWW focus is more on what they are trying to say in writing, and less on the act of handwriting.

5. **Save everything.** Students receive credit for everything they write. If they do not want to continue a first draft, they still get credit for that one draft since abandoning a writing experiment is a choice they have. If they do five drafts, they earn credit for each one. When students are encouraged to experiment, they improve their writing skills.

6. **Date and label everything.** Such identifying of papers helps students keep organized and assists when scoring their writing folders.

7. **Work really hard and make good choices.** So much of what students do in the workshop is done in the classroom; they cannot afford to waste time during the school day. When students are diligent they learn a habit that will serve them well the rest of their lives.

8. **Speak in quiet voices only.** Too much noise distracts other students and also makes it difficult to conference with individuals. The workshop is a place for purposeful conversation about writing; it's not a lunch room.

Students check the writing experiments in their folders as well as look at the ideas on the classroom walls to come up with a topic. Everyone's choice is noted on the list. Students can pass the first time around the circle, but before they leave the class meeting, they must give me a topic, a *starting point* for their writing. If they are stumped, they stay at the class meeting until they make a selection. I nudge, encourage, and, if all else fails, I get them to pick one idea to use as a starting point. If that idea leads nowhere, they can always select another.

Before students return to their desks, paper for first drafts is passed out. They use their writing experiment as a basis for their first draft, but must realize that the writing experiment is not a first draft. A writing experiment is fast, hurried, just a burst of thinking that does not reflect later thoughts, changes, and improvements. In addition, they are to consider the suggestions listed in the Persuasive Writing Guidelines chart. If a new first draft was not required, students would probably say that their writing experiment is their first draft and so they were done. They would then need a conference which I am not ready to do today. Establishing in students' minds that all writers rethink and rewrite is fundamental for the success of this and future workshops. While I write in the center, students write at their desks for the rest of the period.

PERSUASIVE WRITING WORKSHOP GUIDELINES
1. Explain why the change would be a good idea. In the example of a pay phone, students would be able to call home for rides once an after-school activity is completed.
2. Convince the audience that the change will be good for them as well. For example, students would not have to bother the secretaries in the office if there were a pay phone.
3. Anticipate the audience's objections. For instance, if the principal is the audience, he/she might object to students' missing class to phone. A solution to that objection might be that the pay phone is only to be used during designated times. If students can put themselves in the shoes of the audience, they may come up with answers to meet objections.
4. Suggest how to accomplish the change. Students may call the phone company to find out the costs and other considerations.
5. Support your position with personal experiences. If students write about a time that they were stranded after school with no ride home, they will have strengthened their argument for a pay phone.

Tomorrow the first draft is due, and it will be the day for peer response groups. Making a first draft due the next day presses students to keep the ultimate deadline for the final draft in their minds. It also allows me to have most students ready for peer response groups. Deadlines have a magical way of helping students become productive and use their time well. Students with computers are encouraged to take the first draft home and type it in. Tomorrow they can make changes right on their hard copy. Drafting becomes child's play with a computer.

Establishing these classroom routines in the beginning of the year is crucial to the success of future writing workshops. Both classroom management routines and a classroom atmosphere of purposeful work must be in place before effective teaching and student learning can occur.

Day 5

Peer Response Groups

On this day for peer response groups student conversation fills the classroom. Days 5 and 6 of the Ten Day Writing Workshop are set aside for student response to student writing. Peer response groups are concentrated into these two days so subsequent days can be devoted to teacher conferences without major distractions. When the students enter the classroom, their attention is drawn to the posted schedule for the next four days.

Day 5 - Peer response groups

Day 6 - Peer response groups, second drafts, and teacher conferences

Day 7 - Teacher conferences

Day 8 - Teacher conferences, writing due

Today's essential question is: *What is my role in this learning community?* The daily outcomes are to: (1) participate in class meeting, (2) fill out the peer response group sheets (see example on p. 22); and (3) participate fully in a peer response group. After the students "check in," they are reminded that if any member of the peer response group is ready for a peer response conference, all others in the group stop what they are doing to participate. Students waiting for a peer response conferences are invitations for trouble. The Writer's Peer Response Group Worksheet is discussed first.

WRITER'S PEER RESPONSE GROUP WORKSHEET

_____Writing Workshop   Teacher initials this space
                                        BEFORE the PRG begins_____

Writer_____Section_____

Recorder_____   Response Tally-er_____

I. WRITER'S QUESTIONS FOR PRG (about 1. a specific paragraph, 2.
    certain sentences, 3. various words, 4. the lead, or 5. the ending –
    student must pick at least one of the five) In complete sentences,
    write at least one of your own questions.

    A.

    B.

    C.

II. CHECK OFF WHICH QUESTIONS YOU WANT TO ASK YOUR PRG
    Choose at least one to check off.)

    ____ A. Any part you want me to reread because it sounded like I
             was using telling writing, not showing writing.

    ____ B. Where do you want to know more?

    ____ C. What didn't you understand? What questions do you have?

                    **Reread your piece to yourself
                    in a one foot voice before PRG**

            ENTIRE TOP SECTION MUST BE FILLED IN
                 BEFORE THE PRG BEGINS

The purpose of the peer response group is for the writers to receive help in improving their writing. Peer response groups are safe places for student writers. Group members are not to rewrite another's piece since rewriting and making changes are the writer's choice and responsibility. To prepare for the peer response group the writer asks one member of the group to be the recorder and the other to be the response tally-er. Then the student writes one question each for Sections I and II. In Section I, Writer's Questions for PRG, students focus on certain sections of their draft for revision and help. It may be the beginning of the story or the end. It may be about a certain sentence or paragraph that just does not sound right. It may be about a needed word. In Section II, students check off one to three of these questions to ask group members.

Once students have written their questions, they read their piece in a "one foot voice." Brains of students and teachers alike think faster than their hands can write. Consequently, sometimes students forget to write words that they meant to put in their piece. They can best find missing words or confusing passages by reading their piece aloud. When students become skilled at reading in a "one foot voice," they have an invaluable tool for self-editing. When students have completed the writer's sheet, the teacher initials that space in the upper right hand corner of the sheet to check if the writer is truly ready for the peer response group. When the writer is prepared and ready, the time of the other group members is not wasted.

The simple recorder's Peer Response Group Worksheet is depicted below.

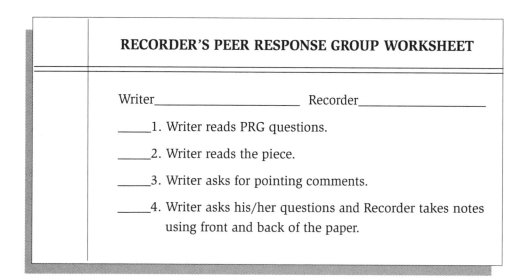

RECORDER'S PEER RESPONSE GROUP WORKSHEET

Writer_____ Recorder_____

_____1. Writer reads PRG questions.

_____2. Writer reads the piece.

_____3. Writer asks for pointing comments.

_____4. Writer asks his/her questions and Recorder takes notes using front and back of the paper.

Peer response groups are safe places for student writers.

Students note that *writer* is the subject in each sentence since the writer controls the peer response group. The others in the group answer the writer's questions and give the feedback the writer needs but do not rewrite the piece. When the peer response group is over, the writer decides what changes to make. During the peer response group, it is the role of the recorder to keep the group on track by checking off numbers one to four as each task of the writer is completed. The Recorder takes notes of the answers given as reminders of what was said in the peer response group.

The response tally-er's worksheet is then explained. On this sheet there is a space for the names of the three members of the peer response group. The response tally-er makes a tally mark anytime the recorder or the response tally-er points, gives an opinion, or answers a question. The tally marks indicate who is participating. The mere act of making marks helps the groups stay on task.

RESPONSE TALLY-ER'S WORKSHEET
Writer_____
Response Tally-er_____
Recorder _____

When the peer response group is completed, the writer collects all three sheets, and staples them together. The sheets will be used by the writer when preparing the second draft. Before students have a teacher conference they write a second draft in paragraphs which includes the changes the writer wants to make. When the second draft is in paragraphs students can see better what parts of their piece need to be developed.

I then read my first draft to the class to use as a model for a peer response group. I go through all four steps listed on the recorder's sheet to demonstrate the elements of the peer response group. This modeling demonstrates the kinds of questions that students might ask their peer response group to elicit the most helpful feedback. Students point and respond to my questions. They help with the rough spots and learn that writing well is challenging for me, their teacher.

After reviewing the status of the class, students are sent out to meet in their peer response groups. My role is to observe body language and check in with them from time to time. I do my best not to interrupt the conversation of the group. Students benefit from hearing the good writing of others as well as learning new possibilities for their own pieces. If individual students are not taking the process seriously, they are reminded about meeting the daily outcome to participate. If that has no effect, they are pulled out of the group for the rest of the workshop. Group members should not be expected to endure an unwilling participant. Unwillingness happens infrequently since students enjoy the opportunity to talk during class time. Yet, not all peer response groups work well. They may go through the peer response group process rather mechanically without giving any useful feedback. For such groups, teacher conferences are safety nets, and provide an opportunity to address problems.

During the first writing workshop of the year more than one day may be needed to explain and practice the peer response group procedures. Time spent learning the routines of the Ten Day Writing Workshop results in more effective and smooth running writing workshops in the future. On this fifth day of the writing workshop it is important to have faith. Slowly, peer response groups evolve into functioning groups. They make school not such a lonely place for students who are new to the school, without close friends, or lack social skills. It takes time for students to be effective responders, but those who learn to give feedback look more thoughtfully at their own writing. In the beginning, it is important to realize that students are learning a structure that will make them better writers. The very structured approach to peer response groups in the TDWW gives students a starting point to learn the skills of discussion and giving feedback. For teachers, peer response groups are absolutely essential for their health and well being. No teacher can meet all the conferencing needs of all students. Successful writing workshops definitely need peer response groups.

Day 6

Peer Response Groups and Teacher Conferences

On this second day of peer response groups, all students who have not had a peer response group have one today. Even if writers' pieces are not completed, they get feedback on this day, since the intent is to hold the engaged conversations to Days 5 and 6 of the TDWW. In addition, the deadline for writing their pieces is only two days away. If students do not have their peer response group on Day 6, they will have a difficult time meeting the Day 8 deadline when writing is due.

The students collect their writing folders and come to a class meeting for "check in." The essential question is *What will I do to improve my writing?* The daily outcomes are: (1) to actively participate in the peer response group, and (2) to write independently on a second draft. Once again I review the schedule ahead.

Day 6 - Peer response groups, second drafts, and teacher conferences

Day 7 - Teacher conferences

Day 8 - Teacher conferences, writing due

The first mini-lesson of the day is on what to do if you have finished a peer response group. When finished with peer response group:

1. Staple the three peer response group sheets together.
2. Decide on changes you want to make and consider the suggestions from your peer response group.
3. Think about rearranging paragraphs and/or sentences to make the piece sound better.
4. Write the second draft legibly in paragraphs.

The second mini-lesson is on paragraphing. Paragraphs begin when a writer:

1. describes a new place
2. introduces a new time of day or week into the story
3. introduces a new subject
4. writes dialog for a new speaker

If students indicate they don't know how to paragraph, they receive an instant teacher conference on paragraphing. If others say they have no changes to make in their first drafts, they are pulled aside for me to skim the pieces quickly. I look to see if there is focus. If so, I check for sufficient development. Nearly always, I find places where students have either not focused or have not developed their pieces fully.

If students would like further response to
their writing after their peer response group
is finished, they may select anyone in the
class with whom to have a peer conference.
The writer gives the piece of writing to the
peer to read as they sit shoulder to shoulder
in a corner of the room. The peer reads
through the entire draft without comment,
but makes *x*'s at the beginning of any line
that is confusing or about which he/she has
a question. Once the peer finishes reading,
the two talk about the writer's piece. The

*Voluntary peer (or pair)
conferences are helpful.*

pair conference meets the needs of students who did not receive much useful
feedback in the peer response group. The peer conference minimizes the frustra-
tion of more able writers who might feel the peer response group has been a
waste of time. Peer conferences are helpful to the writer, for the peer reads exactly
what is on the paper. Sometimes, when writers reread their pieces, their mind
reads words they meant to put in but, in fact, left out. In addition, writers get to
hear what their writing actually sounds like, which may give them new insights
into what they will change in their second draft.

The third mini-lesson is on "showing writing." Students write "Star System
(Show, not Tell)" at the top of their paper. They number from one to seven
putting stars before each number. Then a sentence is read, "She was my favorite
person." What would make a person a favorite person? is asked. After a discussion, the sentence, "He was nervous?" is read. What would someone be doing
who was nervous? is brought up. Telling words are general descriptions without
the specific details that make good writing come alive. Words like *gross, ugly,* and
mean need more explanation. With the permission of a student writer a draft is
passed out that contains telling words, general and non-specific words. Students
star any words they feel are telling, not showing in this piece of writing. We
discuss the student choices and elaborate on "showing" substitutions for these
"telling" words. After a volunteer reads his/her piece, students write down any
"telling" words they hear as the student reads. The class discusses the choices
and the possible "showing" substitutions. Then students review their own pieces,
starring the words that are "telling," not "showing."

After I check the status of the class. students finish any peer response groups
and write second drafts. Though the teacher conference explanation is tomorrow,

teacher conferences are held for anyone who needs one. In the beginning of the year this Day 6 may also take two days, since presenting the mini-lessons to teach students the routines of the writing workshop takes time that won't be needed in subsequent workshops.

The use of peer response groups is a high risk activity. These groups are not as neat, clean, and orderly as worksheets. When meeting with others, students are learning meaningful communication skills. The self-discovery inherent in writing makes students more committed to their own education. Clearly, peer response groups are fruitful for top students. They are given the opportunity to exhibit their incisive and to-the-heart-of-the-matter questions. Such students do not need a teacher to referee at every juncture of their education; they need opportunities to lead and be independent learners.

Day 7

Catch-up Writing Session

The essential question is: *What can you learn from the adults in your life?* The daily outcomes are to: (1) complete a teacher conference, and (2) to write the next draft independently. After the students check in, the chart for taking a piece through the drafting process is explained.

One Way to a Final Draft.
1. Writing Experiment
2. First Draft
3. Peer Response Group/Peer Conference
4. Second Draft
5. Teacher Conference
6. Third Draft
7. Teacher Conference
8. More Drafts
9. Final Draft

This chart reassures students who still seem mystified as to the sequence of the workshop. The mini-lesson is preparing students for teacher conferences.

Students are responsible for signing up for a conference with me. When students are ready for a teacher conference they write their initials on the blackboard under the heading of *Teacher Conferences*. Having initials on the blackboard allows me to see at a glance who is next. Then I move next to that student's desk for the conference to use the time effectively. The desks of the students are separated enough so that my chair can be alongside a student's chair. When the teacher goes to a student's desk and sits at eye level with an individual, a powerful message is communicated. Another way to conference with students is to have them come to the teacher who is sitting at the front of the room facing the class. The conference is held shoulder to shoulder which allows the teacher to give attention to individual students as well as be able to look up occasionally to see how other students are doing. Either way signals that we are partners.

One on one conferences are an integral part of the workshop.

Students not immediately involved in a conference check the chart of ideas depicted on p. 30 to consider while waiting for a teacher conference.

STUDENT PREPARATION FOR TEACHER CONFERENCE

WRITER _____

Before you fill out this sheet read your piece in a one foot voice

This sheet is for a conference about what you are trying to communicate; to determine whether your focus is clear and whether you have given your audience enough information (development). Later conferences will address grammar and spelling.

1. Number of draft _____
2. Focus _____
                  (In one sentence write what the story is about.)
3. What part of the piece do you want me to read? (beginning, middle, end, or certain pargraphs)_____ _____
4. List the questions you want to ask me.
   A.
   B.
   C.

WHILE WAITING FOR A TEACHER CONFERENCE

1. Check your spelling	5. Write a first draft of another piece
2. Check your paragraphing	6. Read from the classroom library
3. Write ten titles for your piece	7. Write a poem
4. Write a new lead	8. Read in your pleasure reading book

After the status of the class is recorded, students return to their separated desks. Often students come to me at this point with questions about their writing or upcoming conferences. It is important that I do not immediately get caught up in meeting these individual needs. Rather, I take a minute or two to make certain all students settle down to work. During this noisy transition from class meeting to working at desks, time is needed to settle the class down. If students do not start to work, the noise level may remain unacceptably high.

For teachers to be able to meet the conferencing needs of all their students, students must be ready when the teacher comes to their desks. My goal is to have each teacher conference last from one to two minutes. Without this self-imposed time limit, it is impossible to meet the conferencing needs of all the students. Further, there just is not time enough to read all of a student's piece nor time for them to read their pieces to me. The information on the teacher conference sheet makes it possible to begin the conference without delay and focus it.

At a student's desk I scan the conference sheet, then skim the section the student wants me to read. I begin by mentioning something good about the piece. Students are anxious and vulnerable during these first teacher conferences, so it is important initially to notice something they do well. After the pointing, students relax and listen to the other comments. I come to these teacher conferences with the following hierarchy of composition skills in my head that students must address.

HIERARCHY OF COMPOSITION SKILLS

1. focus	5. sentence variety
2. development	6. word choice
3. lead	7. voice
4. ending	

In addition to the student's questions on the teacher conference sheet, I first address whether the piece has focus. If there is focus, I check for development. My experience is that focus and development are issues middle schoolers need to address throughout the year. If they are both satisfactorily addressed, I move down the hierarchy to identify those aspects of writing that need attention. Composition skills three through seven are interchangeable to meet individual student needs.

If the focus of a student's piece is not evident, I mention that there are, say, three stories here, and ask the student to choose one. If development is where help is needed, I ask questions to get the student talking about the details of the story. Sometimes I ask them to visualize in their minds the picture of what they are describing. At teacher conferences we address only one issue of composition. Trying to squeeze both a conference on focus and one on development leads to trouble; students often leave such conferences confused and overwhelmed. Issues of spelling and grammar are saved for subsequent conferences.

At a later teacher conference, a hierarchy of convention skills is addressed in this order.

HIERARCHY OF CONVENTION SKILLS

1. paragraphing
2. complete sentences (run-on sentences, end punctuation, capitalization)
3. quotations or agreement of tense or subject-verb agreement

Paragraphing really should be addressed before the first teacher conference, since it is difficult to explain to students the need for development when their writing is not in paragraphs. If paragraphing is in place, sentences are addressed. The conference proceeds to meet specific student needs of grammar and usage.

At teacher conferences I question, nudge, and challenge students to improve their writing in light of their skills and needs. One of my goals for teacher conferences is for students to assume ownership of their writing and control of the conference. Students improve their writing when they see the value of writing well, rather than when they make changes just to satisfy the teacher.

Once a teacher conference is completed, the class list is marked with abbreviations to indicate what was talked about in the conference. For an issue of focus "foc" is written, and for one of development "dev" is noted. If a student were especially engaged in the conference, asking questions, and giving opinions, a star would be placed by that individual's name. Writing on students' papers is avoided and only done with the student's permission. Later, notes help during the scoring process. Day 7 is most satisfying, for it gives me the chance to deal with students one on one, helping them with their individual writing needs. The personal touch of teacher conferences makes students feel valued and willing to risk writing again. In the beginning of the year I keep a half eye on the class while I conference. If there are any students not working, I go over to talk to them individually. For the writing workshop to succeed, good classroom management must prevail.

After School Catch-up Session

At first students assume this session is detention by another name. The after school catch-up session is an opportunity, before writing is due, to have extra time to meet the deadline. Students volunteer for this forty-five minute session which is for writing and conferencing not completed during the school day.

This session makes winners of students, parents, and teacher. Students get the time they need to complete the writing assignment. They score umpteen points with mom and dad for their willingness to stay after school to write. Parents become strong allies for teachers who put in extra time for students. The teacher wins on three counts as well. One, the opportunity to work with students one to one occurs. Two, a few more teacher conferences are completed to lighten the conferencing load for tomorrow. In fact, more time is available for each teacher conference. Three, working with a motivated group of students is a joy in an atmosphere that is productive and relaxed.

Students are not required to come to these sessions. Parents are aware of this after-school opportunity, and it is up to students to take advantage of this time and take more responsibility for their own education. Students usually leave these sessions with a clear idea of what they need to do to make tomorrow's deadline.

Day 8

Scoring Writing Folders

G oals and deadlines are the mothers of productivity. After the "check in," students are drawn to the statement on the blackboard, **Writing is due today.** The essential question is: *What personal standards of quality do I apply to my writing?* The daily outcomes are: (1) write independently, (2) participate in teacher conference, and (3) complete the final check of last draft. Before students scratch their itch to write, mini-lessons on convention are held if needed. Following the rules of grammar and spelling helps to ensure that writing will be understood by any reader.

The punctuation mini-lesson begins with an explanation of how to self-edit for punctuation. One goal of the workshop is to promote independence and the ability to self-diagnose. In time, students develop these skills and no longer need the teacher to come to the rescue. Without punctuation, sentences can be a never-ending trail of information. The audience does not know where the writer is going or where to catch its breath. Pausing when students read their writing in a "one foot" voice is a starting point for learning to punctuate correctly. More often than not, these pauses suggest a need for a period rather than a comma. Students also note sentences that have two or more commas or two or more "ands." It is certainly possible to have a correct sentence with two commas or two "ands," but it is a signal for students to relook at these sentences to be sure they are not run-on sentences. Commas here and commas there afflict many middle school students. Students reread their latest drafts to see where they naturally pause. Often a period rather than a comma is the preferred punctuation.

The **spelling mini-lesson** emphasizes self-diagnosis by the writer as well. Students reread their pieces of writing and circle every word that they are not sure is spelled correctly. Future mini-lessons will suggest strategies for using the dictionary or spelling book to find correct spellings. If students have many spelling errors, they are instructed to find five and correct them. After that I correct all other misspelled words. If poor spellers must find every error, they spend a disproportionate amount of time in the writing workshop correcting their spelling and neglecting other areas of writing. Even more likely is that they become discouraged and give up when facing a mountain of misspelled words.

Students use all the resources they have to improve their spelling. Spell checks on computers and comments from classmates are two such resources. A spelling quiz is given to all my students to identify spelling assistants for each class. Every student takes the quiz as well as lists the names of three students in the class who are both good spellers and approachable, someone they would go to for help with spelling. These lists of seven to ten students per class give poor spellers another option in seeking out help for their spelling woes. Spelling assistants do not correct the words for others, but help identify words that need correcting as well as offer the first letters of a word to get the poor speller on the right track. My students spell better on their final drafts because they are held accountable for good spelling. A final draft with spelling errors is returned as incomplete.

The last mini-lesson is the Final Check explanation. If students feel they have finished, they write their initials under the heading *Final Check* on the blackboard. The final checks allow me to see in the final draft if paragraphs are correct, sentences are complete, and spelling is accurate. Final checks are time savers, for they catch minor errors that otherwise might cause students' writing folders to be returned as incomplete. Once students are done, they staple all the goal writing, peer response group, and teacher conferences sheets together. They in turn staple their drafts together starting with their final draft on top and all the other drafts in reverse order. I can see at a glance the progress students have made through the drafting process, which makes the scoring more effective. Any other writing experiments are stapled together in a third pile. The stapled drafts eventually end up in the students' permanent writing folders.

After I take a check on the status of the class, students begin writing, and I start having conferences. If students have been absent or working diligently and it appears that they will not be finished by the end of the day's writing, they have until tomorrow to complete their writing. Conscientious students deserve the extra day necessary for them to complete their draft. Day 8 is a quiet, focused day of writing. Scoring of the writing folders lies ahead.

After School on Day 8

After school I seize the moment to score as many writing folders as possible. The students' writing is fresh in my mind since I have recently read drafts of their pieces during conferences. In addition, I identify all the incomplete workshop folders. On Day 9, students with incomplete folders will have them returned for completion without delay.

The Scoring Rubric of Performance Outcomes (p. 18) gives students the most complete information possible about their writing. Rubrics are specific as to the students' strengths as well as good for identifying areas that need to be improved. Teachers who do not want to be overwhelmed by the demands of evaluating student writing will find the scoring rubric simplifies, clarifies, and speeds up the task.

Each of the eight categories of the rubric is averaged, molded, and bent in order to come up with a grade that will motivate and encourage students to write in the future. *Basic* is thought of as a grade of *C*, *Proficient* as a *B*, and *Distinctive* as an *A*. Though the skills and habits that students are developing are what I emphasize, students, parents, and administrators still want a grade. (In time I hope they will be weaned from such dependency.) No grade is written on the rubric itself but is recorded in the grade book for the student to see.

If students turn in their writing folder after the deadline, they are dealt with on a case by case basis. If students have been absent, there is no penalty. If students did not use class time well, then their grade is lowered for missing the deadline. Timeliness matters. Students know that if they work diligently, they will have the time needed to complete their writing. If students write longer pieces, they receive a reasonable amount of additional time. If any of the five writing skills of the rubric are incomplete, the writing folder is returned to the student for completion.

Once the writing folders are all scored, it is time for scoring conferences. If all the folders are not scored during my prep period and after school, I hold the conferences a day or two later.

Day 9

Conferencing with Students on Scoring Rubric

Today's essential question is: *Do I value my own opinion when I assess my writing?* The daily outcomes are: (1) to complete the self-evaluation, and (2) to work independently. As the students come to class on Day 9, I look at the class list of names to check in with any students who have not handed in their writing folders. Then the incomplete folders are returned with an explanation of what needs to be done. Class begins with a writing workshop self-evaluation by the students.

_____WRITING WORKSHOP SELF-EVALUATION

Name_____Date_____Section_____

1. What changes have you made from first to last draft?
2. What did you do well in this writing workshop, and explain why you think that?
3. What did you learn from this writing workshop and how will you put that knowledge to use?
4. What are one or two goals you will choose for the next writing workshop?

Once students have spent a few minutes completing the self-evaluation, they are called to a class meeting. After we "check in," students bring their writing folders individually to my desk as we review the scoring rubric together. While I am conferencing with one student, the other students are working on a current events assignment, taking part in a small group activity, or reading silently. It is important that students are focused and purposefully engaged during the rubric conferencing. A chair is placed beside my desk for the next student and an "on-deck" chair by the blackboard for the next student.

When students come to a scoring conference, their strengths are noted first. This too is a vulnerable time for students and must be treated accordingly. When what they have done well is pointed out, they become relaxed in the same way they did in peer response groups. The student's comments on the self-evaluation are discussed, and we decide on one area that he/she might work on during the next writing workshop. The students will have both this scoring rubric and their self-evaluation available when they start their goal writing in the next workshop.

After all the scoring conferences are completed, conferences with any students who have incompletes are held to check on and give them a pep talk. Once I have talked with everyone, I sit back and let them continue to work. Having given my all for this writing workshop, I relax a bit and resist the urge to rush into another class meeting or some other productive classroom activity.

Day 10

Will my audience understand what I have tried to say?

T he essential question for the final day of the Ten Day Writing Workshop is: *Will my audience understand what I have tried to say?* The daily outcome is to publish. After the morning "check in," students copy their pieces for the audience that they had in mind. If the audience is someone at school, students have class time to seek out that person. Often the audience is the principal, the gym teacher, or the team leader. School staff know the students and are gentle in their approach. They take students seriously and can be most encouraging. The principal appreciates the contact with students who are not in trouble. If the audience for the students' writing is in Kittery or elsewhere in the United States, the needed addresses are located.

If a piece of writing is mailed to an audience beyond the school, I review it completely before it is sent. Some people in the community may judge harshly a student piece if there is a misspelling or an incorrectly punctuated sentence. Students should not be judged so harshly that they wither under scrutiny. Student work needs editing when their pieces are going "public." Rightly or wrongly, students, their teachers, and the entire school system may be judged negatively solely on the basis of a misspelled word or a run-on sentence. This is the reality, and so I review any piece before it is mailed.

There are simple and less costly alternatives to the more elaborate book-making form of publishing.

1. Students read their pieces to the class. If students are expected to read their pieces in class, that is stated at the beginning of the workshop. Usually everyone reads, but when pieces are of a personal nature or on a sensitive subject they are not read. Reading aloud is always voluntary. Students who read poorly read their pieces

Speaking before the class develops many critical skills.

just to me. Reading pieces aloud is a day to celebrate writing. Students make invitations to include adults in this celebration as well as bring refreshments to add a festive air to the day. Moms and Dads are still the most popular adults invited by middle schoolers. After the reading of each piece students clap to foster a safe setting for all. When reading aloud students are indeed vulnerable. I want them to be confidenct that I will provide a classroom climate of respect. Not surprisingly, students often read their own writing well. Some students read with flourish, while others make major strides if they just read in front of classmates without falling apart.

2. Student posters. Students choose an excerpt from their story to place on a piece of poster board. Pictures and captions related to the story are added to the poster. This option connects their artistic side with their literary side.

3. Students read their pieces in a lower grade. The sense of pride and accomplishment that comes from reading to an attentive and appreciative audience buoys my students for writing workshops ahead.

Epilogue

What has been described here is an example of a writing workshop. Such workshops are not the means to correct every problem associated with student writing. The workshop's primary purpose is developing students' habits of inquiry, diligence, and quality in relationship to writing. The workshop format provides a setting for students to take their present level of writing to the next level. For the teacher new to writing workshops, learning the skills and routines of the Ten Day Writing Workshop takes some time. My skills, still under development, were honed over a decade. I learned to have a sense of humor about my efforts and to be gentle with myself when things did not go well. I realized that I could only do what I could do, and no more. When I gave up the compulsion to keep on schedule, life was better for me and my students. If we needed two, three, or four more days, we took them. Teacher frenzy kills the best of writing workshops.

The first time through a newly created writing workshop is a learning experience. It's a "first draft." Though the routines of the Ten Day Writing Workshop are time tested, there is no certainty that a new writing workshop will be flawless. During a new writing workshop students teach me what works and what to set aside. I tinker and change the format to meet the specific needs of students, then try out the "second draft" next year. It may take years to finely tune a writing workshop, and it's funny, once that happens, I am usually ready to create a new workshop. One beauty of the Ten Day Writing Workshop is that it allows teachers to teach to their passion. No matter the genre or subject of a writing workshop, teachers can teach the skills of composition and convention.

There are times when I limit the number of pages to three (writing on one side only). Rambling pieces often lack details and foster the myth that "more writing is better writing." Students need to get to the meat of their story. The three page limit reinforces the idea of focus to them. The Ten Day Writing Workshop is not for epic pieces. Students need the feedback they receive from their peer response group as well as the benefits derived from teacher conferences. The time needed to talk over one's writing is impossible to secure when students write page after page. If students want to write more than three pages, they might write a first "chapter" that is limited to three pages, and then write the next chapter independently for extra credit.

This writing workshop excites, motivates, and stirs the writer within most students. Occasionally it does not. The writing workshop is both an opportunity and a privilege that depends on the willingness of students to commit themselves to writing and to allow others that same opportunity. The writing workshop is not an inalienable right. When a student's behavior disrupts the education of others, an alternative for that individual must be found. In those instances, an individual program is organized. Before students are placed into an individual program, we meet to discuss their lack of productivity or disruptive behavior. Students may realize that the freedom of the writing workshop may not be the best setting for them to learn. Once students describe their impression of the situation, they are made aware that they may be placed in the individual program. If this initial conversation does not result in a change in behavior, we set up an individual program. Students in an individual program work at desks to the side of the classroom and do not have the freedom to move about the classroom during the writing workshop as the other students do. They are not to talk to others nor are others to talk to them. The teacher is the sole instructor for these students as they work on the same writing assignment as all the other students.

On the first day a student follows an individual program, a class meeting is held with the rest of the class to explain what is going on. The option of an individual program is not offered at the beginning of the year since it may not be necessary. When students are placed in the individual program, parents are notified of that change. Each day students are in the individual program, they earn a grade for their work habits and productivity. The grades are *P* for poor, *S* for satisfactory, and *X* for excellent. Students have twelve days in which to earn six grades. When students earn them, they are eligible to return to the regular writing workshop. If students do not earn the needed grades in twelve days, they begin a new cycle of twelve days in an effort to earn six excellent grades.

Once students have earned the needed marks, we have a conference about returning to the writing workshop. They are asked what they might do to help themselves return to the writing workshop. A commitment from the students that they are willing to be productive and cooperative is necessary. It is possible that students and teacher will agree that remaining on the individual program is the appropriate choice. For a very few students the freedom of the writing workshop is too much, and the individual program better fits their needs.

All in all the Ten Day Writing Workshop offers a manageable way to help students improve their ability to write, and for teachers it provides a structured program of accountability. ✎

—2—
After Writing Workshops

Although writing workshops are the foundation of my language arts classes, week after week of workshops is a routine that would wear my students and me down, sap our energy, and, over time, dull our commitment to writing. We all need a change and a different sort of challenge. Born of this need and desire, students have additional workshops in public speaking; they memorize and recite, discuss in class meetings, and collaborate in small groups.

Public Speaking for Middle Schoolers

It was a cool mid-fifties January morning in Tempe, Arizona, when I arrived at Carroll Lovebury's fifth grade class at Mitchell School to be introduced as the new student teacher. Within minutes, perspiration circles around each armpit soaked my buttoned down shirt as I trembled at the thought of speaking to these ten year olds. After Carroll introduced me, I told a few stories about myself, they asked a few questions, and eventually my sweat glands calmed down. In fact, after a short while, I quite enjoyed being the center of attention. Who wouldn't?

Middle schoolers are no different. Initially, their fear of speaking in front of others immobilizes them. Their self-imposed limits keep them from achieving the advantages of the well spoken – influencing others, becoming leaders, and maturing confidently. For students to develop as public speakers, they need teachers who structure the classroom for success, provide many opportunities for practice, and create a safe classroom atmosphere. Given enough opportunity, students get over their nervousness and love the attention and validation public speaking gives them. Their self-esteem builds with the recognition that comes with speaking before others.

Students are expected to speak in front of their classmates twenty to thirty times during the school year. Speeches are a starting point to reach that goal. Speeches require students to organize information, present the information in a clear and orderly way, take risks, and ultimately gain self-esteem. For each speech, students have three opportunities to speak before classmates. First, there are mini-lessons on eye contact and enthusiasm to be practiced in front of classmates. Then there is a day set aside to practice their speeches. Finally there is the speech day itself.

Five speeches are scheduled per year. There is no substitute for guided and repeated opportunities to improve public speaking skills. The year begins with the *Artifact Speech* which allows students to talk for just one minute on an object, some personal artifact that is meaningful to them. This mini-speech allows students to take the first swing at breaking through their fear of getting up in front of classmates. The *Demonstration Speech* in which students perform or demonstrate a skill they possess is a good second speech since they already know the information about which they will speak. They organize the speech and use props to teach their classmates. Mid-year the *Memorable Incident Speech* about a meaningful event in the students' lives is assigned. Again, all the information that will be presented comes from the experiences of students. The fourth speech is a recitation of Martin Luther King Jr.'s *I Have a Dream Speech*, emphasizing the public speaking skills of pausing, inflection, and gestures. In the spring, the *Storytelling Speech* pushes the students further. In storytelling, they create characters, setting, action, and resolution themselves. Those additional challenges involving their writing skills are an appropriate culmination to a year of speech making.

Speeches allow for the continuing development of many critical skills. *Decision making* by students after reviewing speech options is necessary. There is the opportunity for *creative thinking* as students consider how to entertain and engage their audience. *Organization* in preparing for the speech carries over to other assignments and tasks. *Independent learning* comes with the planning students must do on their own to complete their original speech. The *collaboration* and *cooperation* among classmates in the preparation of the speech promotes interdependence and highlights the advantages of learning from others. Obviously, *verbal communication* is at the heart of the speech-making experience.

The demonstration speech workshop provides an excellent starting point for learning about how to organize speeches. For this workshop, the outcomes are limited since sufficient time to practice and develop these skills is needed. Outcomes are to organize information to meet a deadline and to speak enthusiastically while making eye contact. On the first day of student preparation the daily outcomes likewise are succinct to focus the students' attention on what they need to do to succeed. They are to listen and support the speaker, to participate in the class meeting, and to brainstorm ideas for a teaching speech. The essential question is *What wisdom do I have to share with others?*

To hook the students, I begin the workshop by giving a juggling demonstration. My willingness to risk encourages students to risk themselves. When I speak with animation and seem to enjoy myself, students begin to rally around this idea of public speaking. Once finished juggling, I hand out the Demonstration Workshop Information Sheet along with the Demonstration Scoring Rubric (p. 44).

DEMONSTRATION WORKSHOP INFORMATION SHEET

Task: How to make something or how to perform a job or a skill

Workshop Outcomes: Organize information in an understandable way and speak effectively in front of others.

Expectations: Create a title card which includes the objective (How to...), a picture related to the topic, student name, teacher name, and date due. Bring in props related to the topic and a note card with notes that show in what order the speech will proceed. Speak for five to seven minutes.

Suggestions: Use parents and friends as a source of ideas for your speech. Original and unusual subjects are favorites with audiences. Cats, dogs, large animals, weapons or items that could be used as weapons (e.g., guns, arrows, knives) are unacceptable as speech topics. Lead off the speech with a story since people of all ages love stories. Consider using volunteers from the audience. Practice your speech at home and prepare for it to last five minutes. If you have samples of food, bring in enough for everyone. If necessary, be prepared with extension cords.

Due Dates: Idea_____

Practice Day_____

Demonstration_____

Each section of the Demonstration Workshop Information Sheet is reviewed. The note card helps speakers organize their thinking and provides a safety net if they forget what they had planned to say. Sufficient practice and preparation allow speakers to relax so they can be enthusiastic and make eye contact. Students then brainstorm possible subjects. To spark their thinking the categories of

DEMONSTRATION WORKSHOP RUBRIC

Name_____Section_____

Incomplete	Basic	Proficient	Distinctive

1. EXPLANATION

| ___ minimal | ___sufficient details | ___detailed description, stories | ___many details, with examples and tips, stories |

2. VISUALS AND PROPS

| ___careless work, misspellings, too small, hard to read | ___legible, correct spelling, uniform printing | ___legible, correct spelling, variety of lettering, well organized | ___legible, correct spelling, colorful, details, creative organization, distinctive appearance |

3. EYE CONTACT

| ___none or little | ___most of time | ___always, takes in whole audience | ___always, takes in whole audience, eyes dance |

4. ENTHUSIASM

| ___smiles little, stands in place, few gestures | ___smiles, gestures, body movements | ___smiles, appropriate gestures and body movements, has fun, speaks up | ___smiles, dynamic gestures and body movements, has lots of fun, dynamic volume |

5. TIME

| ___under 3 minutes or over 7 minutes | ___3 to 4 minutes | ___4 to 6 minutes | ___6 to 7 minutes |

HABITS

1. Inquiry

2. Diligence

3. Quality

_____
Reviewer

ADDITIONAL FACTORS   ___met deadline   ___student additions

44

sports, hobbies, jobs around the house, clubs and organization, arts and crafts, instruments, animals, and preparing food are suggested. Before students leave for the day, they select a leading choice.

For the second day of preparation students write a story that relates to what they will be demonstrating to their classmates. Once done, the students write on a piece of paper their demonstration topic starting with the objective (How to...). Sitting in a class meeting circle students then pass this paper to the classmate on their right. That student looks at the objective, and then on the bottom line of the paper writes one question he/she would like answered about the topic. When this first wave of students have written their questions, they fold the sheet up from the bottom to the back, hiding the question. On signal, they pass their sheets to the right for the next student to write another question about the topic. Students continue to fold their question back under and pass the papers to the right until the papers return to the speakers whose topic is listed at the top. These questions give students a host of ideas to consider as they prepare their speeches.

During the third day of preparation a lottery is held to assign dates on which students will make their speeches. A lottery reduces student grumbling because it is fair and random. One inch oaktag squares equal to the number of students in a class are numbered so that one-third of the squares have a *1* on them, another third have *2*'s, and the final third have *3*'s. The bag is shaken and students select a square. The *1*'s go on the first day, the *2*'s the second, and the *3*'s the third. Students then fill out the Demonstration Workshop Worksheet, collaborate with a peer, and organize their speeches. As the students work, I check to see if anyone has an individual question that would help him/her in preparing.

As the demonstration workshop enters its fourth day, students work on their first and second drafts of their title cards. At a class meeting prior to creating the title cards, students are reminded that passing around props to the audience during the speech is a distraction. Students are also encouraged to bring a watch on speech day to keep track of the time. While the students work on their title cards, I hold conferences with students. The questions below are used in discussing their upcoming speech.

1. What is your demonstration about?
2. Your speech is due _____. Do you think it will last 3-5 minutes?
3. What props are you using?
4. Is there anything I can do to help?
5. Do you have someone at home in front of whom you can practice?

6. Are you going to be using volunteers from the audience?
7. What story are you going to tell?

DEMONSTRATION WORKSHOP WORKSHEET

Name_____Section_____

I. How to_____(the topic)

1. What are two or three key points that you want your audience to learn when you give your speech?
2. What problems did you have as you learned this skill?
3. How can you involve your audience in your demonstration?
4. List the visuals you will need to bring on the day of your speech. Will you use handouts?

II. Peer Conference

1. Student reads and explains the information on his/her demonstration workshop worksheet.
2. Peer points, then conversation begins.
3. Peer answers questions, tells where he/she would like to know more, suggests possible trouble spots, and ask questions.

III. Planning the Speech - On the back of this paper list in order what you will say as you demonstrate. Later refine these notes and put them on an index card.

The fifth day of preparation is the practice day. Before students go off to different spots in the classroom to practice, I "treat" them to two speeches. In the first, I make all the speaking mistakes in the world to emphasize what not to do. Then, I blow them away with a dynamite speech. Next I outline on the blackboard what happens in each peer response group for this day of practice. First, the speaker speaks, then the speaker asks for pointing comments. The group members point out what was good, great, creative, funny, or interesting about the speech. Group members then give feedback to the speaker on whether he/she was enthusiastic, making eye contact, speaking loudly and clearly enough, and using the three minute time minimum. In turn, each student gives his/her speech to the others in the small group. Practice day is a wake-up call for students who have not prepared sufficiently. The lack of preparation is obvious to both speakers and classmates. The pointing in the groups boosts the confidence of the speakers for the risk-taking day ahead.

For demonstrations, desks are placed against the wall and the chairs arrranged in audience seating which creates an earnest atmosphere to the day. A stage is set up in front and another in back. While one student is speaking in the front, another is setting up in the back. When one speaker is finished students turn their chairs around. This arrangement minimizes the downtime between speeches and keeps the class on schedule. A student volunteer tapes the title cards to the wall for each speaker. I sit behind the audience to maintain eye contact with the speakers so as to nod and encourage them as they speak. If students are just not making eye contact, I interrupt briefly to remind them to look up. If students are not prepared for their speech, they sit facing the far wall to use the time to plan and prepare for speaking tomorrow. If students say they forgot their props and claim they are not ready to speak, they are told that the show must go on and do what they can. If students are not successful at speaking the first time or are just petrified, they speak their second time just to me and a few friends. For my special needs kids, a feeling of success in speaking is more important than making the three minute time minimum.

As for scoring, the rubric has clarified expectations from the first day. Further explanation of the elements of the rubric is done at teacher conferences during the preparation time of the workshop. If students are incomplete in any one category, they do the entire speech again; a second time for the class, any subsequent efforts are done for just a few chosen classmates and me. The demonstration workshop is a wonderful "gifted and talented"-type assignment for *all* students since the format allows students to work and perform to their ability. Students can challenge themselves and draw upon their talents to delight and entertain their classmates.

When students come to a conference with their demonstration workshop rubric, I tell them what they did well. At some point in each conference I often mention how adequate preparation is the key to success in public speaking. This experience is meant to be a positive one, so I end the conference with words of encouragement. In addition, they know they will have another opportunity to improve their speaking skills during the next speech workshop.

Teachers should be gentle with themselves as they evaluate their own initial efforts at organizing a speech workshop. If teachers think they could have done more to help students achieve, it is important to remember that it is not any one teacher's responsibility to take students "the whole way." Faculty colleagues who know about the ongoing workshop, support the effort, provide related practice, and otherwise collaborate. We as teachers take students as far as we can go during the year that we have them. Sometimes growth is slow. There are factors beyond our control such as family situations, student maturity, and community issues that greatly affect how much influence any one teacher or team of teachers can have in helping a troubled or unwilling student. Next year, other teachers will pick up where the present teachers have left off.

One major benefit of speeches is what they do to build a sense of community within the class. Students know more about each other and feel more connected. They are no longer anonymous once they have given speeches. Finally, almost all of the teacher's work during the speech workshops is done during the school day. Teachers score the speeches as the students deliver them. Rubric conferences happen during the school day as well. Speech workshops allow teachers the time to renew and recharge for an upcoming writing workshop.

Recitation Workshops

In September students approach recitation in a variety of ways. Some students trudge to the front of the classroom as if the guillotine awaits. Their eyes plead for mercy. When no mercy is forthcoming, their shoulders hunch and their heads sag. Others whine, *I'm not ready. I can't do it. I didn't get a chance to study. This is stupid*, in the hope they will say the magic words to sidetrack the teacher, while others wave their hands wildly, volunteering to go first. Some start their recitation by closing their eyes and mouth in the apparent belief that any opening in their head might cause the words to seep out and escape forever. Others have their parents write notes of excuse in a futile effort to evade personal responsibility and buffalo the teacher. Let's acknowledge the obvious. Young adolescents are adolescents. Teacher resolve and good humor in the face of student creativity and evasion are critical in setting a foundation for developing good speakers. Once students have physically taken that momentous first step, however haltingly, and are in front of classmates, they are on the road to public speaking success.

Student resistance to speaking before classmates is heartfelt and widespread. Students need many opportunities to melt their fears away. Recitation complements speech workshops in developing students' speaking skills as well as building their self-esteem. In order for recitation to be a positive learning experience, teachers must create a safe setting as well as hold students accountable for their part in their own learning.

At the end of the year, students feel somewhat differently about reciting, as these comments indicate.

> *At the beginning of the year I was scared to death to get up in front and speak. I am more comfortable with it now and my face doesn't turn red when I do it (or so my friends tell me).*

> *Well, I was afraid to talk in front of the class, but now I love to.*

Of course, there are some dissenters.

> *I got worse because I used up my memory.*

During my second year as a teacher I introduced recitation to fourth graders. The fact is, it was born of a need to help me fill up the six hours a day I had with my thirty students. In desperation, I came up with the old idea of having them recite the *Gettysburg Address*. No principal could question such a patriotic curriculum choice. Over the next two weeks my students grew to like the attention that reciting brought them. Since then I have modified and expanded the use of recitation. The recitation is often the first step in using the memorized poems, stories, and speeches to introduce writing workshops or prepare for acting in mini-plays. Over time the many reasons I've compiled for memorizing and reciting come to light (p. 52).

Desiderata (1952) by Max Ehrmann is an example of a poem that is used to teach the skills of memorizing and reciting. Max Ehrmann's advice on living introduces an "Advice Giving" writing workshop. The performance outcomes for a recitation workshop are: to organize time to accomplish the task of memorizing, to begin to speak smoothly in front of an audience, and to chip away at the students' speaking-in-front-of-groups phobia. Three to four days is often the length of any memorizing and reciting workshop. I have found that students put off preparing to recite until the last minute anyway. Two nights to study gives them ample time to memorize the short sections of a piece they must recite. If students have been working diligently and need more time to successfully recite, they always know they will have enough time to succeed.

ROTHERMEL'S REASONS FOR MEMORIZING AND RECITING

1. Preparing to recite promotes self-discipline and is a means of challenging oneself.
2. Students may be asked to memorize facts and formulas in school and in life. Quick recall saves time in most jobs. It requires an active, not passive mind.
3. Successfully reciting helps students develop self-confidence.
4. Reciting is an opportunity for students to become more comfortable in front of classmates.
5. Reciting is an opportunity to show determination.
6. Reciting develops a sense of community within the classroom since the students share the same challenge and experience.
7. Reciting and feeling what it is like to be in front of an audience develops empathy for others.
8. The memorizing selections are examples of good writing.
9. Reciting is an opportunity for students to change their reputation by showing classmates how well they can do with a challenging assignment.
10. Reciting allows students the chance to excel in a very visible way.
11. Memorizing requires the development of organizational and planning skills. Preparing to recite helps students learn to set goals and use their time well.
12. The memorizing selections can be used effectively to introduce a unit of study or a workshop.
13. The recitation day makes for an exciting school day. It gives the student an opportunity to be both dramatic and the center of attention.
14. Successful reciting requires adequate preparation. Reciting well is very difficult to fake.
15. The selections to recite teach vocabulary in context.
16. Preparing to recite provides an opportunity to collaborate with others in completing a task.
17. Preparing to recite is an opportunity to develop the habits of inquiry, diligence, and quality.

On the first day of preparation for reciting the assignment is introduced by the question of *why memorize?* After the students exhaust their ideas, copies of Rothermel's Reasons for Memorizing and Reciting are passed out for discussion. After the discussion, copies of *Desiderata* or other selection are passed out.

DESIDERATA

1. Go placidly amid the noise and haste, and remember what peace there may be in silence. As far as possible, without surrender, be on good terms with all persons.

2. Speak your truth quietly and clearly; and listen to others, even the dull and ignorant; they too have their story. Avoid loud and aggressive persons; they are vexations to the spirit.

3. If you compare yourself with others, you may become vain and bitter, for always there will be greater and lesser persons than yourself.

4. Enjoy your achievements as well as your plans. Keep interested in your own career, however humble; it is a real possession in the changing fortunes of time.

5. Exercise caution in your business affairs, for the world is full of trickery. But let that not blind you to what virtue there is; many persons strive for high ideals, and everywhere life is full of heroism.

6. Be yourself. Especially do not feign affection. Neither be cynical about love; for in the face of all aridity and disenchantment, it is as perennial as the grass. Take kindly the counsel of the years, gracefully surrendering the things of youth. Nurture strength of spirit to shield you in sudden misfortune.

7. But do not distress yourself with imaginings. Many fears are born of fatigue and loneliness. Beyond a wholesome discipline, be gentle with yourself.

8. You are a child of the universe, no less than the trees and the stars; you have a right to be here. And whether or not it is clear to you, no doubt the universe is unfolding as it should.

9. Therefore be at peace with God, whatever you conceive Him to be. And whatever your labors and aspirations, in the noisy confusion of life, keep peace with your soul. With all its sham, drudgery, and broken dreams, it is still a beautiful world. Be careful. Strive to be happy.

— *Max Ehrmann*

The recitation rubric is handed out to clarify the performance outcomes for the full recitation experience. Recitation is another opportunity to develop the habits of inquiry, diligence, and quality that are the foundation for a successful life.

RECITATION RUBRIC

Name_____Section_____

Incomplete	Basic	Proficient	Distinctive
1. PRODUCTIVITY			
___ sections 1, 2, 3, and 8 not all completed	___ sections 1, 2, 3, and 8	___ sections 1-5 and 8	___ entire poem
2. DELIVERY			
___ hesitates, misses words	___ no hesitation, 1-2 transpositions	___ smooth and even, accurate, inflection	___ flowing, accurate, animated
3. EYE CONTACT			
___ none or little	___ most of time	___ always, takes in whole audience	___ always, takes in whole audience, eyes dance
4. GESTURES AND MOVEMENTS			
___ stands in place, no or few gestures	___ some gestures and body movement	___ appropriate gestures and body movement	___ dynamic gestures and body movements

HABITS

1. Inquiry

2. Diligence

3. Quality

_____
Reviewer

ADDITIONAL FACTORS   ___ met deadline   ___ student's own additions

The vocabulary of *Desiderata* that is unfamiliar to the students is reviewed in a class meeting. Students are offered an "early bird" option to recite (part but not all) for the class on the second day of the workshop, a day ahead of when the reciting is scheduled. "Early bird" reciters help other students see that the memorizing assignment is possible. Students who recite a day early derive a great deal of satisfaction and positive feedback by completing the recitation ahead of time. If the "early birds" do not recite correctly, they are aware of what parts they need to review for regular recitation day.

After the vocabulary review, attention is drawn to the charts on the classroom wall listing all the students in previous years who earned a distinctive rating for reciting the entire *Desiderata*. After every reciting workshop, a chart of the students who recited the entire assignment goes up on the wall. Typically fifteen to twenty names appear on each chart. Year after year these charts remain on the walls of my classroom serving as motivation for my present students as well as a touch of "immortality" for students from years past. Since my present students know many of those listed on the charts, they can feel, "If they can do it, so can I." In addition, these charts keep me connected, in a small way, with my former students. High schoolers return to see if I really did continue to hang those charts with their names on them. When I meet former students in town, they often smile and say, "I remember when we memorized ...," and then rattle off a favorite passage.

Next, without a minute's delay all the students are asked to stand. They begin reading the first three sections chorally. More times than not, the choral reading is restarted since middle schoolers often begin quite timidly. To further motivate them, students are told that when my hand is at waist level they are to read the piece in a normal speaking voice. When I raise my hand, they speak loudly, even yell. As my hand lowers to the floor, they whisper. This technique whips them into a frenzy in no time. Sometimes, the class is divided into two sections. First the right side recites one line of the speech, then the left side recites the second line. The two sections go back and forth until the piece is finished. Just for fun, we sometimes sing whatever piece we are memorizing to a tune such as *Old McDonald Had A Farm*. It turns out to be great fun, and makes students' first association with memorizing this year positive.

Students offer suggestions about how they will study at home. One idea is marking key words with a highlighter and repeating an initial phrase or sentence until it is remembered, and then adding the next phrase and sentence. Reading the poem five to ten times into a tape recorder, then lying back in bed listening to the tape over and over is a favorite technique. Some believe that studying just before bedtime and immediately upon awakening are excellent times for retaining memorized passages. Also, students are encouraged to take their memorizing paper with them wherever they go throughout the day. Whether in the car or before dinner, students can catch moments to study. Studying for ten to twenty minutes at a time may be more productive than hunkering down for two hours the night before the recitation day. Students are encouraged to study their words precisely since initial mistakes are often imprinted in their brain and difficult to change.

With the remaining time in the period of this first day students select a partner with whom to study. Partners practice, rehearse, and test each other. Before students leave for the day, they are asked who they will study with tonight to set them thinking about the night of preparation ahead. As with the initial writing workshops, teachers may find that the preparation and explanation require two days to complete rather than one.

On the second day, after the "early birds" recite, students are reminded that there is an "extra help" session after school for anyone who feels that they need more time to prepare for the recitation tomorrow. Then a discussion begins on the meaning of various sections of the poem, and the advice of *Desiderata* is related to the lives of middle schoolers. Over the last ten minutes of class students work with a partner to prepare for tomorrow's reciting. Students leave class with a few more sentences memorized to serve as a foundation for the night's studying. While students are preparing, two chairs are set by mine in the center of the classroom for any student to conference with me about the upcoming recitation. The classroom is quieter and more focused than the day before as the reality of standing before classmates sinks in. Tomorrow is the practice day when they will be asked to recite the first two sections, speak smoothly, make eye contact, use gestures and body movements.

The third day of preparation gives students an opportunity to practice in front of classmates. First, I recite *Desiderata*, demonstrating three of the elements of the rubric: delivery, eye contact, and gestures and body movement. Then students go in front of the class to recite the first two sections of *Desiderata* themselves. Once students finish reciting, students in the audience say what they liked and what suggestions they had for the reciters. Once students have spoken up I comment on the reciters' successes and what they might work on as they practice tonight. Those students who are not prepared get a "wake-up" call about what they must do to be prepared for tomorrow.

Prior to the start of class on recitation day, students place all the chairs in an audience setting to provide an appropriate atmosphere. I ask for volunteers to go first and put those initials on the blackboard. Soon all the other students' initials are added to the list. An on-deck chair is placed for the next reciter to minimize the time between recitations and maximize the opportunities for students to recite. When students are reciting, I prompt them once, if necessary, with a phrase to get them restarted. I do lots of nodding and "thumbs up" to support the reciter and thank each one by name when they finish. After every successful effort the entire class claps with gusto. When they finish, students are called back to my desk when they finish for congratulations or an explanation of what they still must do to complete the assignment. Throughout the class period, if students want to raise their rubric rating, they can recite as often as time allows.

If students are unprepared, they go to a corner of the classroom to study. There is no sense wasting everyone's time with someone who is not prepared. If students are unsuccessful after an initial effort, they select a classmate who has already completed the assignment to help them study. Students have as many opportunities as they need throughout the period to complete the reciting. When students are going slowly, it is often a tip off that they are not prepared. Even when excuses come hot and heavy, students are expected to do as much as they can. Even if it is only five words, they get to experience what not being prepared feels like. Calls are made to parents of students who receive an *I* for the recitation. Parents learn that their child has another day to complete the assignment, and, if necessary, can work after school to prepare. When the recitation workshop is done, students generally are quite pleased with themselves over their success. Students earn self-esteem by reciting.

Throughout a school year four to six of the suggestions listed below are chosen for recitation workshops. Teachers can teach to their passion and to their students' interests when selecting passages for recitations.

1. In September, reciting the lead paragraphs of Ernest Hemingway's "Old Man at the Bridge" is assigned. His descriptive lead helps students visualize what they are asked to memorize. Students recite only the first four sentences to earn a Basic rating since the goal for the first recitation is for the students to succeed and be willing to try the subsequent more difficult recitations.

2. Later *Desiderata* by Max Ehrmann is assigned to introduce an "Advice Giving" writing workshop. A variation on this "advice giving" is to have students interview their parents or an important adult in their lives. They write an

introduction to read to classmates about that person, then recite the words of the selected adult.

3. To introduce a poetry writing workshop students memorize three lyrical poems by Langston Hughes, "Vari-colored Song," "Negro Servant," and "Refugee in America." Another reciting variation to introduce a poetry writing workshop is to have students select the poems for classmates to recite .

4. Midyear, to coincide with the Martin Luther King, Jr. holiday, students memorize his "I Have A Dream" speech. Once they have memorized King's words, they recite as if giving the speech; emphasizing pauses, gestures, and inflection.

5. Students memorize the passage from the play, *The Diary of Anne Frank*, the suspenseful scene near the end of the play when the phone rings and the residents of the attic argue about whether to answer it or not. Once the students have memorized, they choose classmates help in acting out this scene with props.

6. In preparation for a writing workshop on the elderly, reciting the wisdom of Nadine Starr, age 85, in "If I Had to Live My Life Over" is assigned.

7. In preparation for a playwriting workshop students form groups of three and recite a classic play adaptation. Choices include *Shipwreck* by Ambrose Bierce, *The Lady or the Tiger* by Frank Stockton, *Little Girls Wiser Than Men* by Leo Tolstoy, *The Celebrated Jumping Frog of Calaveras County* by Mark Twain, and *The Upheaval* by Anton Checkov.

8. During a writing workshop on the "Dilemmas of War" in conjunction with the social studies teacher, the American Civil War is used as a case study. To introduce this writing workshop, the reciting of the *Gettysburg Address* is held. Students may dress up as Abraham Lincoln, Mary Todd Lincoln, Tad Lincoln, a nurse, or a soldier to give this speech. To each successful student, a shiny new Lincoln penny is given.

9. The rhythm and pace of Henry Wadsworth Longfellow's "The Midnight Ride of Paul Revere" make it a favorite of students who like to show off their recitation skills.

The year ends with students preparing for the middle school exhibition for reciting (see Chapter 3 for the full listing of middle school exhibitions). For this exhibition they recite a poem, speech, or piece of literature. Once finished reciting, students explain its meaning to them and why they chose this piece of writing.

Class Meetings

Phoenix, Arizona. When I think back to my first days of teaching, I remember staying late after school trying to come up with enough things for my sixth graders to do to keep them busy the next day. As a teacher in a self-contained classroom, I had to plan for everything; math, reading, spelling, social studies, science, and health. During that time I was under the impression that if I did not know what to do, I should pretend that I did. I hid my self-doubts from colleagues and felt totally responsible for all the learning that went on in the classroom. Therefore, I tried to control everything. I directed from the front of the class, motivating and entertaining my students while at the same time handling the discipline without the need of a principal. Clearly, I was working harder than any of my students and quickly driving myself out of the teaching profession. Most days I left school exhausted, weary, and wondering.

As I was hitting bottom, good fortune came my way from California. William Glasser in his book, *Schools Without Failure* (1969), opened my eyes to the reality that students had as much responsibility for their education as I had. My responsibility was to create a positive classroom atmosphere for learning while theirs was to become actively engaged in their own education. For students and teachers to reach that end, Glasser suggested class meetings. It sounded good to me, and I had nothing to lose. To start off I drew my twenty-eight students to the center of the classroom in a class meeting circle. In the beginning class meetings were kept to ten minutes because I was afraid I might lose control. I did not, and kids soon warmed to a structure that actually encouraged them to talk, a novel idea in the 1970s. The fact is students paid more attention because of the intimacy of the circle since there were no desks filled with items to play with nor a "back of the classroom" where students might "check out." In addition, class meetings added variety to the day and required me to keep on my intellectual toes. Within days, I knew I was on to something good.

Class meetings are well-suited to teaching those verbal communication skills that young adolescents need. Kids need a setting in which to listen and speak appropriately. They should learn to respect one another in discussions and have a forum in which to ask questions and state their beliefs. They need to learn to support their opinions with reasons and facts and to stay on the subject (to focus) during a discussion as well as how to ask follow-up questions. The ability to hypothesize and thoughtfully reflect should be developed. All of this requires a setting wherein they can articulate what they think. Class meetings ideally provide such opportunities. No matter the discussion topic, be it questions about why the Nazis would murder Jews, how to respond in a peer response group, how to brainstorm speech ideas, or discuss problems in the lunchroom, class meetings allow the give and take of meaningful communication. The greatly varying prior knowledge that students possess keeps discussions fresh and less predictable from class to class. This variety keeps teachers who direct several heterogeneous classes stimulated and challenged. The extemporaneous nature of class meetings gives teachers and students fresh possibilities each day.

The classroom arrangement greatly affects the success of the classroom community and the learning of communication skills. The thoughtful set-up of desks and chairs can encourage discussion and minimize classroom management issues. To leave a ten by fifteen foot open space in front of the blackboard for class meetings, clusters of three desks are set around three sides of the classroom. Even when space is tight, it is worth the time and effort to move the desks back to the walls in order to have the space for a class meeting circle.

The class meeting starts with "a check in" when students have a chance for one to four minutes to bring up subjects of their own, often unrelated to the lesson at hand. "Check in" allows students to ask questions and make comments before the daily lesson begins. In the beginning of the year, students often do not know what to make of this "check in." Little is asked or said by the students as they wonder what is going on. In time, a few hardy students risk a question or an opinion or some bit of news, and that is all it takes to get the ball rolling. The regularity of the "check in" gives students a definite time when they can address their own issues and questions.

Students come to class meetings with three items, pen or pencil, lined paper, and something hard to write on. Though they do not always use these three items, they are prepared to write if need be. Students quickly learn to write legibly on their laps. Whatever writing they do at class meetings is considered first draft writing and treated accordingly. Students' participation in class meetings is noted by making check marks on the class listing of the students' names. At class meetings students sit wherever they choose. As a class we developed the following class meeting guidelines that show respect for each other and ourselves.

1. listen and speak in turn
2. make eye contact with whomever is speaking
3. raise your hand if you cannot hear the speaker
4. keep your hands to yourself
5. no put-downs or sarcasm

My role is crucial in reinforcing these guidelines. Insults, negative joking, and name-calling sabotage the positive community-building atmosphere that class meetings create. Once disrespected, students shut down and fold up, rarely to be heard from again. My middle schoolers push and test me on the guidelines until the line is clearly drawn so that they understand I do mean what I say about respect. Discounting and disrespect are unacceptable, period.

When students are disrespectful or disruptive, they are sent to sit apart from the class meeting, against a wall, or at a desk away from the circle's edge. This move provides me with an in-class "time out" space. Such students still listen to the discussion and instruction, but for this one day no longer actively participate. It is wrong to sacrifice the education of students to the disruptive few. Not surprisingly, most students hate to be away from the action of the class meeting and will often do what it takes to return to the class meeting the next day. The removal from the class meeting is for one period only. Tomorrow is a new day for us all. The next day I hold no grudges, but smile, nod, and welcome them back into the class meeting. If the disruption continues, students begin the Individual Program which has them working away from the class center for the next two weeks.

Since class meeting subjects range from here to there, they allow teachers to capitalize on many teachable moments while students are learning the skills of communication. Class meetings provide verbal students a place to shine and succeed while those less verbally adept have opportunities to develop their speaking skills in a safe setting. Class meetings refresh and stimulate student and teacher alike. They challenge teachers to think on their feet and make days in the classroom lively. They are a godsend.

Small Group Work

Ask yourself, what do students need from school? As you think about this question you probably will mention they need the opportunity to:
1. feel safe,
2. learn skills that apply to everyday life,
3. develop habits to help them lead a happy and successful life,
4. learn to respect themselves and others,
5. think critically and creatively,
6. read and write,
7. develop self-confidence and self-discipline,
8. have a place to succeed daily,

9. think for themselves,
10. be challenged and stimulated,
11. work together,
12. get individual attention,
13. produce quality work, and
14. develop a sense of community and a feeling of belonging.

William Glasser in *The Quality School* (1992) suggests that schools become meaningful when they provide students an opportunity to meet these needs:

1. survival (security),
2. love (friendship),
3. fun,
4. freedom, and
5. power (gaining and maintaining respect).

Whether we agree with these needs or not, conversations about what students need and how teachers might provide for those needs create a stimulating and meaningful atmosphere in schools for both students and teachers. Far too often in public schools, teachers dominate and control the interaction and communication in their classes. Students are reduced to a passive role of note taking, completing worksheets, and being tested on the temporary acquisition of information. Sadly, many teachers have neither the time nor the interest to have these thoughtful conversations. Their days are not structured to allow it, administrators rarely promote it, and the teacher's need for autonomy discourages it.

When these conversations among colleagues do occur, teachers can reflect and reevaluate the teaching and learning that goes on in schools. These discussions lead to teaching the critical skills of:

1. decision making,
2. problem solving,
3. communication,
4. leadership,
5. cooperation/collaboration,
6. documentation,
7. creative thinking,
8. critical thinking,
9. management,
10. organization, and
11. independent learning.

Learning such critical skills is basic for students in order to become responsible, productive, and informed citizens in a democracy. Small group work in combination with other classroom experiences helps students learn these essential skills. These critical skills are "real world" workplace competencies that all students need. Try to think of a job that does not call for workers who can cooperate and collaborate. Communication skills enable workers to be productive and success-ful. Creative and critical thinking flourishes in any business or organization that succeeds. Organizing information, making decisions, and solving problems stimulate all involved and create solutions. To master these critical skills students need abundant opportunities in the classroom to develop them.

When teachers use small groups, it is important that the task be specific and clear to the student. When explaining the task to students, teachers first explain the purpose of the task and how it connects to their lives. Initially, students in small groups need tasks that they complete in ten minutes or less. In time, as students develop their small group skills, longer tasks are assigned. In the begin-ning teachers need to go slowly and take the extra time necessary for students to understand the structures and routines of small group work. In group work, roles for each member are clearly defined and purposeful. Without a purposeful role for students during small group work, their commitment and engagement is compromised. Depending on the task at hand, these roles might include *secretary,*

presenter, checker that all agree, keeper of the task, artist, chart maker, or *timer.* Rotating the roles among the group mem-bers is necessary for the full development of small group skills for all students.

Small groups help students learn specific skills.

To organize the small groups, index cards with student names on them are shuffled in an obvious way in front of the class so they do not think that the index cards have been manipulated. Students are reassured that these current small groups are only groups for the duration of the task or workshop. When it is time for the next small group work, cards are shuffled again and students are randomly assigned to new groups. In time, students find the shuffling does not subject them to the traditionally contrived groups that occur when teachers place a high, middle, and low student in each group. In such small groups, high performing students may feel burdened by having to carry the group, again. Low students may resent the know-it-allness and controlling nature of the high ones. Middle level students wonder why they never get to be with their best friend. By shuffling the cards, students have the opportunity to learn from all of their classmates. It is unlikely that future employers will ask students to approve the others with whom they will work.

When assigning small groups, the first three index cards are drawn off the top of the deck to be the first group. The next three names on the index cards are in the second group, and so on. If three generally low-performing students get in one group, so be it. There is an opportunity for leadership and accountability among the three that does not normally occur. If there are four index cards with students' names left at the end, generally two groups of two are made, rather than a group of four. The more students in a group, the more difficult is the learning of group skills. In the beginning, it is important that students are successful, and smaller numbers make that more likely to happen.

If the groups are struggling, I do my level best to avoid butting in and "solving" their problems. Group members need to grapple and squirm a bit as I observe before reluctantly intervening. Working and dealing with people who are not friends is all a part of life in the world beyond school. A blocked or ready-to-come-to-blows group needs teacher mediation to help resolve their specific problem. Groups that are clearly going down the tubes are broken up. If students prove unwilling to participate satisfactorily in small groups, they are assigned to the Individual Program which has students working by themselves.

In September the structures and routines of small group work are taught and reinforced. Regular group work is necessary for students to acquire skills that will serve them well in their lives. Each small group assignment is organized with performance outcomes, task, small group roles, materials, and the clearly delineated time frame. A bonus question is included for those groups that complete the task sooner than the others. As for grading, students' performance is measured against the daily outcomes. Once a group grade is assigned, each group member's grade is raised or lowered based on their individual efforts during the group work. Students' commitment to small group work is jeopardized if their grade is held hostage by an uncooperative group member.

Small Group Work Example #1

Mathematics Slips into Language Arts class

Performance Outcomes
1. To communicate
2. To collaborate in creating word problems
3. To make connections between mathematics and language arts

Task - Write three word problems (using a different arithmetic operation for each one) on separate index cards using the number given below.

1. Problem #1 must use addition with the numbers 16, 47, 83, and 65.
2. Problem #2 must use subtraction with the numbers 16,483 and 13,567.
3. Problem #3 must use multiplication with the numbers 12 and 225.
    Bonus problem #1 must use division with the numbers $3290 and 14.
    Bonus problem #2 is one entirely of the group's creation.

The answers will be new numbers not listed on this explanation sheet. Students can only use the numbers given. The guidelines for the word problems are:

1. They must include the name of at least one of the teachers on the Eighth Grade Team. The references to people must be positive.
2. They must include a location within Kittery, Maine.
3. They must be written on the blank side of the index card and the answer and the "work" on the lined side. The answer must be labeled (e.g., miles, pounds, etc.).
4. The names of the group members must be put on the side of the index card with the answer.
5. The conventions of grammar and spelling are to be attended to so there is no misunderstanding of the problem or the answer.

Small group roles

1. A checker to make sure all the conditions to the activity have been met.
2. A recorder to write the problem, the answer, and the "work" clearly and correctly.
3. A presenter to explain the word problems to the entire class.

Materials - Five index cards per group

Time - Ten minutes

Small Group Work Example #2

To tap the collective wisdom of the class, small group work is set up to promote thinking by brainstorming. The example here asks students to come up with ways to aid memorization. Since students are preparing for a recitation workshop this task is both relevant and brief, conditions that encourage commitment and success.

Memorizing. How is it Possible?

Performance Outcomes

1. To brainstorm ten ideas how one might learn to memorize.
2. To collaborate in completing the task on time and involving everyone in the group.

Task - List ten methods students might use to learn to memorize effectively.

Bonus - List eight careers in which the workers are helped if they have memorized certain information.

Small group roles

1. A secretary to record the list.
2. A keeper of the task to insure that the small group stays focused.
3. A presenter to read the list to classmates.

Materials - One sheet of white lined paper per group

Time - Six minutes

Small Group Work Example #3

This example of small group work is one of a series of assignments to prepare students for an Anne Frank Writing Workshop. Students choose to publish a part of a personal journal or diary or writing fictional accounts after examining pictures of Nazi Germany. In preparation for the writing workshop students view the film, *Diary of Anne Frank* or read *The Diary of a Young Girl.*

It's Never Easy

Performance Outcomes

1. To make decisions on the fate of the eight occupants of the Secret Annex.
2. To think creatively in explaining the reasoning behind the group's decisions.

Task

PART I - Assume Kraler and Miep know that the Gestapo is very suspicious that the spice warehouse is being used to hide Jews. As Kraler and Miep plan the escape for August first, they know that they only have room in their Saab sedan for four of the occupants of the Secret Annex. They will drive those four to a waiting fishing boat on the North Sea.

If you were Kraler or Miep, which four would you select for the escape? Consider who might be useful in the escape and who might be useful if they were left behind. Consider whether you think families should be kept together. Remember anyone left behind is likely to be captured and sent to a Nazi death camp.

Circle *yes* for the ones below you would choose to go with Kraler and Miep and *no* for the ones who would not. In at least one sentence for each person, explain why you chose to take them or chose not to take them.

Mr. Frank *yes no* -

Mrs. Frank *yes no* -

Anne Frank *yes no* -

Margot Frank *yes no* -

Mrs. Van Daan *yes no* -

Mr. Van Daan *yes no* -

Peter Van Daan *yes no* -

Mr. Dussel *yes no* -

PART II - If you were Kraler or Miep, what would you say to the four who must stay? Write the very words, in dialogue form, that you would use to explain why they are not going. Use the back of the paper for your explanation. You might begin, "Please sit down. I have ..."

Bonus - Do you have an alternative to the above escape plan?

Small group roles

1. A recorder for the group's decisions
2. A presenter for Part I
3. A presenter to act out the reading of Part II

Materials - This worksheet

Time - Fifteen minutes

Small Group Work Example #4

To promote a sense of community among the students, our team of teachers uses field trips to support our three day/two night outdoor adventure at Bear Brook State Park near Concord, New Hampshire. Involving the students in a meaningful way in the preparation builds their commitment to the success of this field trip. This preparation also promotes the practical use of the critical skill of collaboration, and reinforces the idea that this is a community where we truly do learn from each other.

A School Day Beyond the School

Performance Outcomes
1. To organize a full day's activities for one hundred eighth graders at a local wilderness area.
2. To write a schedule for the day.

Task - In preparation for the longer Bear Brook Outdoor Adventure, the Eighth Grade Team has set aside one day to visit Mount Agamenticus in York, Maine. Mount Agamenticus is a forested area with hiking trails and a paved road to its summit. Once a ski resort, the mountain top has a fire tower, a boarded up ski lodge, and a rolling grassy area about the size of a football field. The students will leave school by bus at 8:30 AM and return at 2 PM.

Plan a schedule for the day from 8:30 AM to 2 PM for one hundred eighth graders. Include:
1. time for a five mile hike,
2. one hour nature activity,
3. thirty minutes for games,
4. thirty minutes for lunch,
5. one hour for travel to and from Mount Agamenticus, and
6. other appropriate activities for this setting.

Construct a time schedule for all activities. Make a final draft on construction paper. Plan a nature activity of one hour duration using the area around Mount Agamenticus. Make the final draft on white lined paper describing the activity. Consider the size of groups and the activities the groups will be doing. List the games that students will play for at least thirty minutes. Explain your plans to your classmates.

Bonus - Compose a permission slip for parents that includes reassurances that the trip will be safe and educational.

Small group roles
1. A writer of the schedule
2. A writer of the final draft
3. A presenter of the group's plan

Materials - Three sheets of lined paper per group

Time - Thirty minutes

There is variety and unexpectedness in small groups. Students become active and accountable for their own learning in ways they are not often asked to be in traditional classrooms. In small groups, students find that the easy conversations make them feel as if they belong, and school is no longer such a lonely place. Small group work promotes the development of the class as a learning community. Small groups bring balance to students and teachers alike. ✎

—3—
Success-Oriented Grading

G rading is a messy business, full of messy questions.

— What role should effort play in the grading process?

— If teachers deal with students as individuals, then how will they manage the workload of grading one hundred plus students?

— What about national standards?

— If students had to demonstrate their academic competence, would graduation from eighth grade really mean something?

— If students are just "passed on" to the next grade without the skills or work habits to succeed, are not we dooming them to failure in the real world as well as telling them that they can get something for nothing?

— What about grading for work habits? Wouldn't universities and employers want our students to be primarily inquisitive and diligent?

— How do we grade middle schoolers who improve their skills from third to fifth grade level during the course of a school year?

— Since such students are still below "grade level," do they deserve no better than a *C-* or a *D*?

— Does grading lead to unhealthy dependency on others for learning and rob students of the responsibility for their own learning?

The following quiz asks further questions to provoke conversation and reflection about those hated but seemingly eternal grades.

SUCCESS ORIENTED GRADING TRUE/FALSE QUIZ

T F 1. Some kids are just not "A" material.

T F 2. If you do not do something well the first time, you will never do it well?

T F 3. Special needs students do not deserve A's in the regular class if their assignments are modified in any way.

T F 4. You cannot have high standards unless you give some F's.

T F 5. Grading, like life, is not fair. Seeing kids as individuals sounds nice, but fairness is a luxury we just cannot afford.

T F 6. If your students get too many A's and B's, they will not respect you or work for you.

T F 7. As teachers it is our responsibility to cover the curriculum.

T F 8. The teacher is predominately accountable for student learning.

T F 9. If there has been no learning by the students, then there has been no real teaching.

T F 10. If students do not "get" the material that is covered in class, then for the greatest good for the greatest number, the teacher should give the students the low grades they deserve and move on to keep on schedule.

Answers (mine) to the Success Oriented Grading True/False Quiz

1. **Some kids are just not "A" material.** *False.*

   The question is, *Should an "A" reflect a standard of achievement, or should it be a measure of improvement?* Many students are passed onto the next grade with "below grade level" writing skills. Such students who improve a "grade level" deserve the encouragement and satisfaction top grades bring. Conferencing with student and parents is essential in bringing meaning to a letter grade. Without conferencing, it is anybody's guess what the grade really means.

2. **If you do not do something well the first time, you will never do it well.** *False.*

   We all know that "failing" can be a first step in learning. The better question is, *Do we as teachers give students sufficient opportunities to succeed when we assess?*

3. **Special needs students just do not deserve A's in the regular class if their assignments are modified in any way.** *False.*

   As teachers we are here to motivate and encourage learning. If the *A* reflects appropriate growth and improvement, then the *A* is justified. Again, conferencing on grades is a must.

4. **You cannot have high standards unless you give some F's.** *False.*

   We teach so that students might learn. High standards are important, but the firm belief on the part of the teacher that all students can succeed is crucial to student learning. For students to achieve high standards, excellent teaching as well as significant student commitment is necessary. Giving many *F*'s has nothing to do with high standards.

5. **Grading, like life, is not fair. Seeing kids as individuals sounds nice, but fairness is a luxury we just cannot afford.** *False.*

   It is true that life is not always fair, but fair is a worthy goal for all teachers. Fairness is what our students need so they believe that they have a chance to succeed in the classroom. Fairness is not treating students the same, but giving each student the opportunity to learn and succeed.

6. **If your students get too many A's and B's, they will not respect or work for you.** *False.*

   Quite likely the opposite is true if expectations are high and reasonable. Students who see themselves as successful often work to keep that feeling alive.

7. **As teachers it is our responsibility to cover the curriculum.** *False.*

   Covering the curriculum does not mean that the students have learned the course content, let alone been given the chance to work on the critical skills (among them, problem solving, communication, collaboration, and decision making). It is our responsibility to teach the curriculum. Yet, we as teachers have a higher responsibility, that is, to have our students learn and develop good work habits.

8. **The teacher is predominately accountable for student learning.** *False.*

   The teacher is a major factor in the learning equation, but students have primary responsibility for their own education. Parents, too, have a role in supporting good teachers and encouraging their child. The community even has its place in the education of students. Learning flourishes in partnerships.

9. **If there has been no learning by the students, then there has been no real teaching.** *True.*

   Talking at students in a classroom setting without the students learning is not teaching. It is just *talking to students in a classroom setting*. There are circumstances when no learning by students is not the fault of the teacher. Students who are unwilling may not learn despite the best efforts of excellent teachers.

10. **If students do not "get " the material that is covered in class, then for the greatest good for the greatest number, the teacher should give students the low grades they deserve and move on to keep on schedule.** *False.*

    Diligent students of all abilities need varying amounts of time to master both the material and related critical skills. Teachers need to provide more time for willing students to complete their assignments.

It is no secret that teachers hold many keys to the success of students. And several of those keys tie directly to grading. The traditional system sets up many students for failure. There has to be a better way.

Grabbing for straws, I approach Paul Treacy, the school psychologist in Kittery. Sitting in a back booth at Howell's Truckstop on the Route One Bypass, I share my concerns over grading, especially as they relate to my own daughter, Robyn, who attends school in York. Paul asks, "Does York have outcome-based education?"

"I don't know. In fact, I don't even know what that is."

"I have an article by William Spady for you to read."

Our conversation continues as I learn that in outcome-based education teachers first establish appropriate academic outcomes for students, and then they plan lessons accordingly. The performance outcomes allow students sufficient preparation and time to complete the demonstrations of what they have learned. This morning as he speaks the clouds part and the sun shines on me from head to toe. I've hit the daily double. For not only have I found a direction for Robyn's special education meeting, but I have also found a framework to use to reexamine my own middle school teaching, especially after Jayson's speech two days ago.

Jayson is still on my mind later that morning as students come to a class meeting. "How many of you know Paul Treacy?" A few hands rise. "Well, for those of you who don't know him, he's the school psychologist. This morning, Paul Treacy gave me an idea that will make me a better teacher and you better students." Immediately, the words send chills up and down the spines of the students. They look up apprehensively, knowing that a smiling teacher often means trouble. "Today, when I assign the memorizing of the Langston Hughes' poems, you cannot fail."

"What if we can't do it?"

"If you have trouble memorizing and reciting, you will get another chance. If you don't do well the first time you recite, your grade will be *incomplete*, not a *D* or an *F*. In fact, you'll get enough chances to get it right. You will work at study hall or after school, but you'll have the time you need to get it."

Across the class meeting I spot Jayson. He catches my eye, too. I just smile and nod. He wrinkles his brow and bites his lower lip. Jayson was the nudge-over-the-edge that made performance outcomes seem like robins in spring. Two days before, Jayson stood before the class, as all his classmates had done, to give a speech about a memorable incident. As a class, students spent five days preparing for this speech. Ideas were brainstormed on a wide variety of topics. I conferenced with each of them on their selection and had mini-lessons and practice sessions on making eye contact and speaking up. That day as Jayson stood before us, his one hand rested on the desk as he slouched. He smirked at his buddies and shrugged, "I forgot my title card." He looked at me, then to his friends who laughed conspiratorially. He spoke and sputtered for only forty seconds, and then just sat down. The was a smattering of applause, but applause never sounded so hollow and unwarranted as it did that morning. Jayson smirked again. His buddies smirked back.

I looked down at my grading sheet, then back at Jayson. Slumped in his chair Jayson seemed disappointed. Shaking my head, I looked back to his grading sheet on my desk. I wondered how all my efforts to motivate and prepare him led to such a dismal performance. With pen in hand, I had no choice but to fail him. I was going to make sure everyone understood there are consequences for blowing an assignment. I wrote the *F* and called him back to see the grade. From the look on his face I could tell that failing barely registered on his Richter scale.

After school the sour taste of Jayson lingered in my mouth. I looked toward Spruce Creek from my second story classroom window and thought, "Failing kids is not my idea of a good time. It's not what I had in my mind when I went into teaching. What a waste of time this has been for me and for Jayson. I want my students to meet me halfway. I'm not asking for their right arm."

Now, serendipitously, two days later, a colleague gave me a tool to rethink the planning of lessons and workshops. By setting reasonably high standards I make students and myself more accountable. A rubric for a poster presentation is an ideal way to clearly introduce performance outcomes.

If students do not make, say, eye contact, then I pencil in an *I* for incomplete. Later, in conferences, students learn how to make up the incomplete. The student might look at the windows just above the heads of the audience as a first step in making eye contact. Then students find sufficient time to practice, whether at study hall or after school. Calls to parents let them know that the speech was incomplete, but that their child has another opportunity to make up the speech.

Then Marta comes to mind. Three weeks previous, she handed in her final draft for a writing workshop. The final draft had six errors in spelling. "Marta, you said you would take care of correcting the spelling in your piece. "What happened?" I asked.

"I forgot."

"Do you know how to correct your spelling?"

"I forgot."

"Let me show you how to identify spelling errors. Read through your final draft. Anytime you come to a word that you are unsure whether it is spelled correctly, circle it. When you finish circling all those words, come back to me and I'll double check your work."

Marta returns to her desk to correct her spelling. She receives no low grade, but she learns that she will be held accountable for appropriately high standards in writing. It is my responsibility to set up a classroom that allows Marta and all her classmates to succeed. It is their responsibility to address their issues in writing and correct them. If students are just being lazy, they are put on notice that in this class, they will not be able to hand in careless work. Correct spelling is important for it minimizes the possibility that the writing will be misunderstood. If students work diligently and need more time, they get it. Careless student work is often due to the students' belief that teachers will accept just about anything. Teachers will complain about poor work and righteously give it a low grade. Yet, students are safe in the knowledge that teachers rarely expect poor work to be corrected.

EIGHTH GRADER'S RIGHTS POSTER PRESENTATION RUBRIC

Name_____Section_____

	Incomplete	Basic	Proficient	Distinctive
1. EXPLANATION	___ minimal explanation of rights	___ sufficient explanation	___ detailed explanation, connections to adult citizenship	___ many details, creative connections, connections to adult citizenship
2. VISUALS AND PROPS	___ careless work, misspellings, hard to read	___ legible, correct spelling, uniform printing	___ legible, correct spelling, variety of lettring, well organized	___ legible, distinctive appearance, colorful, details, creative organization, correct spelling
3. ENTHUSIASM	___ none or little	___ most of time	___ always, takes in whole audience	___ always, takes in whole audience, eyes dance
4. EYE CONTACT	___ none or little	___ most of time	___ always, takes in whole audience	___ always, takes in whole audience, eyes dance
5. TIME	___ under 3 minutes or over 5 minutes	___ 3 to 4 minutes	___ 4 to 4:30 minutes	___ 4:30 to 5 minutes

HABITS

1. Inquiry

2. Diligence

3. Quality

_____
                                    Reviewer

ADDITIONAL FACTORS	___ met deadline	___ student's own additions

For success, students must believe three things about their teachers.
1. Their teachers care about them and show it.
2. Their teachers hold them to reasonably high standards.
3. Their teachers give them the necessary time to complete their work.

And the greatest of these is that teachers genuinely care.

Guidelines for Success Oriented Grading

A democratic society needs thoughtful, knowledgeable, and ethical citizens to flourish. Schools in American society are expected to prepare students for that responsibility. For students to become such citizens, teachers must believe that all kids can succeed — despite the troubled lives so many children lead. Daily, teachers deal with children of struggling single parents as well as kids from homes where two parents have neither the time nor the inclination to parent properly. Classrooms contain abused or neglected kids from both dismal and privileged backgrounds. There are kids sedated by the drug of television or bought off by the affluence of our time. There are kids who are left alone or who are smothered by well-intentioned parents who have forgotten self-esteem is earned, not given. In many cases, home is not a pretty picture. Like it or not, this is the culture from which many of our students come. We as teachers must be ready for them. Our society needs them to be successful. To be successful, so teachers need to create a classroom atmosphere in which all students experience success every school day. Students' motivation to learn increases when days are filled with success. Success-oriented grading is founded on the belief that all kids can succeed.

Success-oriented grading uses exhibitions and performance outcomes to structure classrooms of success. Teachers determine for each workshop or unit what students should be able to do and what applications to real-life situations students will make. A rubric is then created with specific expectations. Demonstrations allow students to show what they have learned. Discussions with colleagues, professional reading, attending workshops and university courses are among activities and opportunities for reflection that help teachers determine what academic and critical skills students need. Without reflection about what their students are to accomplish, achieve, and demonstrate, teachers can fall victim to teaching lessons because "that's the way we've always done it." Under such a system, the purpose and reasons for their lessons are unclear, random, and superficially connected to the curriculum of the school district. Selecting performance outcomes and exhibitions helps teachers focus on essentials and curb teachers' gnawing guilt that they should "cover it all" when teaching.

Looking back to my tenth grade English class, I remember receiving papers from my teacher with so many red marks (awk, frag, run-on, awk, awk, awk). that I was overwhelmed and most discouraged. I then looked at the grade, hoping it would be at least a *C*. Never thinking I was worthy of a *B*. An *A*? Out of the question. And then, as always, once I had seen the grade, I pitched the paper into the waste basket as I left the classroom. I never knew why I got the grade I did. I didn't know what it would take to improve. It was all a mystery. For my students, rubrics take the mystery out of how their writing is evaluated.

Many students work only hard enough to meet the minimum expectations of teachers. Obviously, teachers must have high and reasonable expectations. Rubrics are written to set such standards. These expectations may be modified to appropriately meet the skill level of both able and less skilled students. Teachers must impress upon students with limited or undeveloped skills that they must work even harder than their academically blessed and able classmates. For less able students, there can be no refuge in excuses and "poor me's." The workplace they will enter wants results, not stories about learning problems. Teachers must avoid creating an underclass of underachievers by lowering expectations for students with learning difficulties. Such students need teachers who hold them to all the elements of success-oriented grading, which includes the responsibility on the part of students to work hard. Expectations must be increased for higher performing students. Such students must be challenged or are at risk to being lost to boredom's dangerous side. We are failing our able students if we allow them to coast through a curriculum that neither stimulates nor challenges them. When students develop the habits of inquiry, diligence, and quality, they are giving themselves the opportunity to succeed no matter their future education and career.

With success-oriented grading, students are evaluated on their exhibitions of learning using rubrics that clearly outline the performance outcomes and developing habits of students. Incomplete ratings indicate that students have not achieved as yet the performance outcomes. Putting aside arbitrary time limits for learning allows students the time needed to achieve competence. Why should diligent students be penalized if they need more time? Isn't the goal of a lesson to have students be able to demonstrate competence? When an assignment is scored *incomplete,* teachers and students both have additional responsibilities — teachers to reteach, and students to recommit to learning. Once students develop the habits of inquiry, diligence, and quality, they are on the main line to success.

In heterogeneous classes it is important to challenge all students of all abilities by offering a self-selected honors program. The self-selected nature of the program gives students another way to challenge themselves. The application to the program outlines the expectations.

Honors Program for Eighth Grade Language Arts

All students in the eighth grade are eligible to participate in an honors program in language arts class. Students who think of themselves as top students or aspire to be such students are encouraged to apply for the honors designation. Honors students complete projects related to the regular classroom work. They also have the option of coming up with alternatives to regular class assignments that follow their special interests. All honors students meet after lunch every two weeks to discuss their progress.

If honors students hand in high quality work, they have both their grade raised in language arts class as well as their honors designation noted on their records sent to the high school. Failure to meet stated deadlines is reason for dismissal from the program. Students may reapply at the beginning of each new school quarter, though honors students in good standing need not apply each quarter. Not surprisingly, honors students are expected to keep up with all the regular language arts assignments.

Once students have filled out the application they conference with me to see if the honors program meets their needs. Each eighth grader who successfully completes the application is accepted as an honors student.

Dan Rothermel, teacher
I, _____, want to be an honors student.
_____ Student Signature/Date
_____ Parent Signature/Date
_____ Teacher Signature/Date
Write fifty to one hundred words explaining why you want to be an honors student.

Exhibitions for Middle School Language Arts

To create meaningful and appropriate performance outcomes for all my middle school students, the following exhibitions are used to show student competency. The students spend the first three quarters of the school year preparing for these exhibitions, then in the fourth quarter they demonstrate their communication skills by exhibition.

By the end of the school year, students will:

1. develop the habits of inquiry, diligence, and quality.
2. write with focus and development as well as attend to the conventions of writing.
3. organize information and articulate it in small and large group settings.
4. develop the critical skills of collaboration, communication, and leadership to improve their problem-solving and decision-making abilities.
5. make connections with their work in the classroom to the "real" world.
6. develop self-confidence to seek out academic challenges.
7. ask questions that get to the heart of the issue.

To demonstrate these communication skills, students will:

1. write autobiographically about an incident or a series of incidents that deal with an important relationship in their lives, be it with a family member, a friend, or an acquaintance.

2. prepare a high school plan. The plan will include:

   a. an introduction about what humanities, sciences, arts, and technologies interest them. They will consider their goals for life and how the high school years will help them achieve those dreams.

   b. an explanation of how extracurricular activities and working in the private sector during the high school years fit into their plans. Further, they will write whether college has a place in their lives.

   c. a schedule of classes for ninth grade that includes an explanation for their choices.

   d. a presentation of the high school plan to an adult for feedback and conversation. Students will write a reflection on the conversation they had with the adult.

3. in self-selected pairs, explain to the incoming class about the eighth grade and what new students will need to do to succeed. Students will relate stories about incidents from the past year to support their conclusions.

4. recite a poem, speech, or piece of literature. Once finished, students will explain the meaning and why they picked the particular piece of writing.

5. in randomly selected small groups, students will develop and present a plan for a community service project. The project will include:

   a. an introduction about the project, supplying a rationale for the project.

   b. a timeline of tasks that need to be accomplished to implement the project.

   c. a presentation to classmates using charts, diagrams, and other visuals to explain the value of the community service project and how it would be organized.

6. in self-selected pairs, lead a ten to fifteen minute discussion on a current events issue in a class meeting setting. Students will:

   a. provide copies of the current event article for classmates.

   b. create an essential question that sparks the discussion.

   c. have their classmates write for ten minutes about the issue after the discussion.

   d. evaluate the written responses and write up their findings.

   e. write an assessment of the class meeting discussion, their learning, and what they would do differently if given another opportunity.

Students are encouraged to seek out the teacher when questions arise during the process of preparing for these six exhibitions. Exhibitions will be evaluated as *incomplete, basic, proficient,* or *distinctive.* Students wanting to raise their score can have conversations with the teacher on how to go about doing that.

Success-oriented grading is a transition step toward the eventual elimination of letter grades altogether. Once administrators, teachers, students, parents, and the community at-large are weaned from grade dependency, teachers will use rubrics for conferencing and as starting points for conversations with parents and student about student performance, progress, and development. At a future date, students will earn credit for completed work based on competency in performance outcomes, and receive incompletes for that work that is in need of revision and improvement.

Once students see themselves as successful and capable, teachers are well on their way to making the classroom truly a learning community. Effective learning communities allow teachers to be able to teach and students to be able to learn. When the following nine characteristics of a successful learning community are supported in schools, classrooms become places where students want to be.

Characteristics of Successful Classroom Learning Communities

1. They have teachers who extend the personal touch. Developing a successful learning community in the classroom starts with teachers who show students that they are personally welcomed into the classroom. In the beginning, teachers who smile, nod encouragingly, and use student names begin to create a bond with their students. Making one or more connections sustains and nourishes students and teachers alike, in good times and bad. Teachers who achieve rapport listen more than they talk. They see the humor in many of the actions of middle schoolers. Teachers who show their students a whole person, one who laughs, is slow to anger and respects others, create classrooms of students willing to enter into a learning partnership. Of course, the personal touch is most difficult with large classes, but nonetheless worth pursuing. When teachers notice students as individuals, they reduce the loneliness which is at the root of so many of the discipline problems in the classroom.

2. They have teachers and students who demonstrate mutual respect. When teachers daily set the tone that they expect students to respect themselves, each other, and the property of the classroom, students acquire a foundation for learning and succeeding. Teacher talk about respect is for naught if teachers do not give the respect to students that they expect. When they respect students' abilities to learn and solve problems and resist playing the seductive role of Answer Man or Answer Woman, students become resourceful independent learners.

Since students are asked to be vulnerable by reading their writing and speaking in front of small and large groups, teachers who read their writing to their students and give the speeches they ask of their students become models of thoughtful risk takers. When issues arise, teachers who problem solve with their students, as William Glasser suggests, develop students who seek solutions rather than point the finger of blame. When teachers use the collective wisdom of the class, they create a classroom community that validates all the members, teacher and students alike.

Once teachers and students agree upon rules of the classroom, then all of teacher and student energy can be geared toward student learning. Souhegan High School in Amherst, New Hampshire adopted seven school rules for teachers and students to create a meaningful learning community.

1. Be on time and be prepared to succeed.
2. Tell the truth; get beyond denying and lying.
3. Treat others as you would like to be treated by them.
4. Be appropriate; know when to do what, where.
5. Respect and encourage the right to teach and the right to learn at all times.
6. Be responsible for your choices; expect to be held accountable for them.
7. Be engaged; ask questions and seek solutions.

3. They have teachers who define performance outcomes and use rubrics to assess them. When teachers determine what students should know and be able to do once a workshop or unit is completed, teachers then create lessons to help students reach those goals. When teachers come to class with performance outcomes in mind, they are better prepared to think on their feet, problem solve as the unexpected arises, and modify lessons in progress to address the rhythm and flow of the class.

4. They have teachers who build dependable structures and routines in the classroom. When teachers list the schedule for the day on the blackboard they prepare students to anticipate what lies ahead. Teachers who begin each class with a "check in" or similar opportunity that allows students a few minutes at the start of the period to talk about issues and questions have better-focused students for the remainder of the class. Daily class meetings allow the development of the classroom learning community and give students regular opportunities to practice the skills of discussion. When students know long-term plans and the deadlines, they can focus their energy and be productive in meeting their responsibilities.

5. They have teachers who create engaging lessons and workshops. Classrooms that allow students to write, speak, plan, and create during the school day engage most students. When students discuss in small and large group settings, they give personal meaning to the content of the workshop. When teachers debrief their students after a workshop, students feel valued and become more thoughtful. When teachers are willing to risk in their writing and public speaking as they expect their students to, they develop students who will risk themselves to achieve quality work in the classroom.

6. They have teachers who establish classrooms that connect curriculum with students' lives. Connecting workshops to students' lives allows thoughtful teachers to take their lesson planning one step beyond mere classroom practice. Once workshops are completed, teachers ask students why they think the activity has value and what meaning it might have to them beyond the classroom. Students often do not really know why teachers ask them to do what they do in the classroom. Student commitment to learning increases when students know why lessons are important and what meaning the lessons have to them personally.

7. They have teachers who believe all students can succeed. Good teachers come to school with an attitude; an attitude that all students can succeed and that as teachers they will structure and individualize the learning environment so that happens. The workshops and units must be structured so that there is latitude within the assignments to both challenge top students, yet allow the less able the opportunity to succeed. Every student deserves a legitimate shot at *A*'s and *B*'s. When teachers build on students' successes and triumphs, student commitment to learning increases.

8. When teachers and students commit to learning and are held accountable, teachers and students both need to be held to high standards. Scoring rubrics help teachers clarify the behaviors and skills they are looking for their students to demonstrate. For students, rubrics clarify what needs to be done. Rubrics take the guesswork out of grading. Teachers must prepare meaningful and thoughtful lessons while students are expected to submit quality work. When students do not, teachers give them opportunities to rework their assignments until they demonstrate quality. When student work is graded incomplete, not failing, students see a classroom that provides opportunities for success. Teachers that expect students to continue working until they reach quality do not let students give up on themselves with shoddy, self-disrespecting efforts.

9. They have parents who are involved. Parents that are aware of what is going on in the classroom become full-fledged partners in education. Regular phone calls home take time but reinforce to parents that they are a needed and wanted factor in the learning triangle with teachers and their child. When the first call to parents is of good news, this initial connection lays a foundation for dialogue for any subsequent calls, be they of a positive or problem-solving nature.

When problems do arise with students' behavior that threaten the learning community in the classroom, despite the best efforts of dedicated teachers, the wisdom of William Purkey is most appropriate. He suggests that teachers first decide whether the student behavior is a concern. The realization that it is not a concern often "handles" many problems. If student behavior is a concern, then it is time for teachers to confer with students by offering three plusses (things students have done well) and a wish of what they want students to do in the future. This one to one opportunity allows teacher and student to problem-solve together. If that does not change the behavior, it is time to consult as to why the previous plan did not work. If the behavior problems continue, then it is time to confront by telling the student the consequences of continued misbehavior. Teachers and students both lose if they reach step five, combat. Students who find meaning and acceptance in the classroom do not become discipline problems.

Teachers who balance their professional, family, and personal lives have the energy and the commitment for their students. When students feel a sense of pride, that deep seated feeling that commitment, engagement, and quality work matter, the world is a beautiful place for one and all. ✎

*Writing workshops involve many
student/teacher conferences.*

BIBLIOGRAPHY

Atwell, N. (1987). *In the middle.* Upper Montclair, NJ: Boynton Cook Publishing.

Bensman, D. (1987). *Quality education in the inner city - the story of Central Park East schools.* New York: The Center for Collaborative Education.

Coles, R. (1989). *The call of stories.* Boston: Houghton Mifflin Company.

Collins, J. (1987). *The effective writing teacher.* Andover, MA: The Network, Inc.

Deford, F. (1983). *Alex - the life of a child.* New York: Viking Press.

Ehrmann, M.. (1948). *The desiderata of happiness.* Boulder, CO: Blue Mountain Arts, Inc.

Elkind, D. (1981). *The hurried child: Growing up too fast too soon.* Reading, MA: Addison-Wesley Publishing Company.

Eppig, P., Mobilia, W., and Monether, P. (1990). *The critical skills classroom.* Keene, NH: Antioch/New England Graduate School.

Fiske, E. (1991). *Smart schools, smart kids.* New York: Simon and Schuster.

Fletcher, R. (1993). *What a writer needs.* Portsmouth, NH: Heinemann.

Frank, A. (1952). *The diary of a young girl.* New York: Pocket Books..

Frankl, V. (1959). *Man's search for meaning.* New York: Pocket Books.

Freedman, S. (1990). *Small victories.* New York: Harper and Row.

Glasser, W. (1965). *Reality therapy.* New York: Harper and Row.

Glasser, W. (1969). *Schools without failure.* New York: Harper and Row.

Glasser, W. (1990). *The quality school - managing students without coercion.* New York: Harper Perennial.

Glasser, W. (1993). *The quality school teacher.* New York: Harper Perennial.

Goldberg, N. (1986). *Writing down the bones.* Boston: Shambhala Publications, Inc..

Gordon, T. (1974). *Teacher effectiveness training.* New York: David McKay, Company.

Holmes Group (1986). *Tomorrow's teachers.* East Lansing, MI: Michigan State University.

Holmes Group (1990). *Tomorrow's schools.* East Lansing, MI: Michigan State University.

Jersild, A. (1955). *When teachers face themselves.* New York: Teachers College Press.

Kearns, D., & Doyle, D. (1988). *Winning the brain race.* San Francisco: ICS Press.

Kidder, T. (1990). *Among schoolchildren.* New York: Avon Books.

Kozol, J. (1992). *Savage inequalities.* New York: Harper Perennial.

Lickona, T. (1991). *Educating for character: How our schools can teach respect and responsibility*. New York: Bantam.

Lortie, D. (1975). *Schoolteacher: A sociological study*. Chicago: University of Chicago Press.

Peters, T., & Austin, N. (1985). *A passion for excellence*. New York: Random House.

Rief, L. (1992). *Seeking diversity*. Portsmouth, NH: Heinemann.

Romano, T. (1992). *Clearing the way*. Portsmouth, NH: Heinemann.

Rothermel, D. (1991). *Sweet dreams, Robyn*. Omaha, NE: Centering Corporation.

Sewall, G. (1983). *Necessary lessons - decline and renewal in American schools*. New York: The Free Press.

Sizer, T. (1984). *Horace's compromise: The dilemma of the American high school*. Boston: Houghton Mifflin.

Sizer,T. (1984). *Horace's school: Redesigning the American high school*. Boston: Houghton Mifflin.

Strunk, W., & White, E. B. (1979). *The elements of style*. New York: Macmillan Publishing Company.

Taylor, R. (1994). *Strengthening English and social studies curriculum*. Bellarie, WA: Curriculum Design for Excellence, Inc.

Ueland, B. (1987). *If you want to write*. Saint Paul, MN: Graywolf Press.

Van Oech, R. (1987). *A kick in the seat of the pants*. New York: Perennial Library.

Wigginton, E. (1985). *Sometimes a shining moment*. Gardner City, NY: Anchor Books.

Wood, G. (1992). *Schools that work: America's most innovative public education programs*. New York: NAL.

Zinsser, W. (1988). *On writing well*. New York: Harper and Row Publishers.

NATIONAL MIDDLE SCHOOL ASSOCIATION

National Middle School Association was established in 1973 to serve as a voice for professionals and others interested in the education of young adolescents. The Association has grown rapidly and now enrolls members in all fifty states, the Canadian provinces, and forty-two other nations. In addition, fifty-three state, regional, and provincial middle school associations are official affiliates of NMSA.

NMSA is the only association dedicated exclusively to the education, development, and growth of young adolescents. Membership is open to all. While middle level teachers and administrators make up the bulk of the membership, central office personnel, college and university faculty, state department officials, other professionals, parents, and lay citizens are also actively involved in supporting our single mission – improving the educational experiences of 10-15 year olds. This open membership is a particular strength of NMSA.

The Association provides a variety of services, conferences, and materials in fulfilling its mission. In addition to *Middle School Journal*, the movement's premier professional journal, the Association publishes *Research in Middle Level Education Quarterly*, a wealth of books and monographs, videos, a general newsletter, an urban education newspaper, and occasional papers. The Association's highly acclaimed annual conference, which has drawn over 10,000 registrants in recent years, is held in the fall.

For information about NMSA and its many services contact the Headquarters at 4151 Executive Parkway, Suite 300, Westerville, OH 43081, TELEPHONE 800-528-NMSA, FAX 614-895-4750.